THE NEW ELECT

MARTIN TIERNEY

THE NEW ELECT
The Church and New Religious Groups

VERITAS PUBLICATIONS 1985

First published 1985 by
Veritas Publications
7-8 Lower Abbey Street
Dublin 1.

Copyright © Martin Tierney, 1985

ISBN: 0 86217 186 5

Acknowledgements
The Author and Publishers are grateful to the following for permission to quote from their copyright material:
The Irish Times, The Irish Press, Irish Independent, Evening Herald, Evening Press, The Sunday Press, Sunday Tribune, The Standard, The Guardian, The Furrow, New Covenant, Theological Renewal, New Creation, The Irish Catechist, Doctrine and Life, The Tablet - the international Catholic weekly, *The Wall Street Journal, Contemporary Christianity, The Clergy Review;* The Pilgrim Press, Dean Hoge, *Converts, Dropouts, Returnees;* Evangelical Protestant Society, Seamus Mulligan, *The Charismatic Controversy;* Addison-Wesley Publishing Co., Hadden and Swann, *Prime Time Preachers;* Seabury Press, Leon Joseph Suenens, *A New Pentecost;* Stephen B. Clark, *Building Christian Community* (published 1972 by Ave Maria Press); Clarendon Press, Ronald Knox, *Enthusiasm* Notre Dame Press, Douglas Hyde, *Dedication and Leadership;* Doubleday & Co., Conway and Siegelman, *Snapping* Pan Books Ltd, William Sargant, *Battle for the Mind;* The Executors of the Estate of William Somerset Maugham, *Don Fernando;* Beacon Press, Bromley & Shupe, *Strange Gods - The Great American Cult Score;* Routledge and Kegan Paul, Roy Wallis, *The Elementary Forms of the New Religious Life,* and Bob Mullan, *Life as Laughter: following Bhagwan Shree Rajneesh;* Daniel Markham, *Cults and Cultism;* Delta Books, Conway & Siegelman, *Snapping;* Robert Dellinger, *Cults and Kids;* Sheldon Press, Thomas Merton, *Seven-Storey Mountain,* NCR Cassettes, Richard Wood, *Cults and Sects - An Assessment;* Dr John J. Roche of Linacre College, Oxford.
While every effort has been made by the Publishers to contact and obtain permission from owners of copyright material quoted in this book, if any involuntary infringement of copyright has occurred sincere apologies are offered and the owner of such copyright is requested to contact the Publishers.

Cover design by Angela Young
Printed in the Republic of Ireland

Contents

	Page
Preface	1

PART I
IN SEARCH OF A SHEPHERD

1. New Religious Groups — The Irish Experience	5
2. The Born Again Christian Groups	13
3. The Born Again Christian Groups and The Church	31

PART II
THE NEW ELECT

4. Personal Testimony	43
5. The Characteristics of Cults	51
6. A Catalogue of Cults	66

PART III
STRATEGY

7. Parents and Cults	91
8. The Church and Youth	102

APPENDIX I
Western Bishops' Lenten Pastoral 1983: Renewing our Faith in the Church — 109

APPENDIX II
The European Parliament and Cults — 114

Bibliography — 117

PREFACE

It is nearly five years ago now since Michael and Joan, a middle-aged married couple, came to consult me. Their daughter Jane had joined 'some sort of religious sect'. That was how they put it. They went on to say that Jane had decided to jeopardise her whole career by abandoning her nursing course. In addition she now intended marrying outside the Church. 'Could I help'? they asked.

This book has been germinating since that first meeting with Michael and Joan. In the intervening years I have had occasion to meet many parents with a similar problem. It is out of those meetings that I became aware of the need for further information and practical guidance. I am also aware that priests up and down the country have been called on to give pastoral guidance in an area that is unfamiliar to many of them.

The fragmentation of religious groups into more and more diversified forms has bewildered and repelled many traditional followers of the major faiths. In Ireland this fragmentation has only just begun. Over the past ten years an increasing number of non-denominational Christian groups and what are popularly called cults and sects have arrived in Ireland 'to carve out a share of the spiritual market', as one commentator put it. These new groups, impelled by a crusading zeal view Ireland as mission territory.

The primary purpose of the book is to inform. Some groups have been unfairly caricatured. Accusations of mind control, brain washing and kidnapping have been levelled at groups who are trying to convince others that their way of life is correct. Admittedly some groups do use subterfuge and deception. Like other zealots, they presume to know what is best for us, better than we do ourselves. Many of the groups are hostile to the values and aspirations of the existing mainline Christian denominations. In order to confront the challenge presented by these groups the first indispensable weapon is accurate information.

One reason why the new religious or quasi-religious groups can gain converts is the high level of ignorance among Roman Catholics about what precisely the Church teaches. With this in mind I have presented briefly the Church's teaching in areas of special concern. It often surprises me how easily young people abandon their faith in favour of another set of beliefs without having an adequate appreciation of what they are leaving behind.

One of the main purposes of this book is to offer practical guidance to parents and pastors. They are the ones who have to deal with young people who become involved in new religious groups. At the moment many responsible people adopt an attitude of benign tolerance. 'Just a fad like hula hoop' they comment. But if joining these groups is a fad, experience has shown me that few who join return to their original starting point. They seldom return to the practice of the faith.

Others adopt an attitude of belligerence. They level charges of serious misdemeanour against what they clearly do not understand. The young people are pilloried and an atmosphere inimical to a charitable solution to their problem rapidly develops. Lives, all lives, are precious. The pastoral approach to be followed by parents, teachers and priests is critical to the spiritual welfare of young people.

The first part of the book deals with the 'born again' Christian groups who have arrived in Ireland in recent years. These evangelical Christians do manifest a deep personal commitment to Jesus Christ. This commitment is frequently demonstrated in a life lived for God. The fact that as Roman Catholics we may disagree profoundly on theological issues does not mean that we can attempt to deny them the right to evangelise or seek recruits. Unfortunately some groups have already been labelled cults and sects. This is unfair. It is these groups that present a particular challenge to the Church. They have been included in this book simply because they are numerous, new, and are having considerable success in attracting adherents.

Finally, I would like to think that *The New Elect* will provide guide for young people. It is written as an expression of the Church's pastoral concern for them. They are the Church of the future and under God the future of the Church lies with them.

MARTIN TIERNEY
March, 1985

1

NEW RELIGIOUS GROUPS — THE IRISH EXPERIENCE

It was curiosity that drew me to the *ashram* in a north Dublin suburb. I had met some wide-eyed, fresh-faced youngsters in the city that day. They were wearing lapel buttons extolling the merits of a certain 'Maharaji Ji'. Who was he, a pop star perhaps? A courteous enquiry brought a rapid rejoinder in rich Dublinese. 'Janey, Father, you don't know what you're talking about. You haven't got the perfect knowledge'. Through this chance encounter I was invited to *satsang*, the evening assembly of the disciples of the Divine Light Mission. *Ashram* seemed a grand title to give to this 'tickey-tackey' dwelling. I later learned that *ashram* meant a holy place of spiritual endeavour.

My first surprise was in being asked to remove my shoes as soon as I entered. I sought no explanation and none was offered. I was led into a room fragrant with incense, at one end of which a large photograph of a beaming sixteen year old Indian youth gazed with innocent charm on the twenty or so young people squatting on the floor. Then the music started. It was powerful and moving. Despite myself I found I was entering into the buoyant atmosphere of hope and love. Hymns were sung and chanted. Jesus was mentioned, but only as a purely historical figure. It was obvious that the young people were 'turned on'. Deep gestures of respect were shown to the photograph of the beaming 'guru'. Is this some sort of a spiritual hula-hoop, a passing fad, I asked myself? What's going on anyway?

In the early seventies I was chaplain at Dublin Airport. At that time my presbytery was often used as a left luggage cum restroom by the 'Children of God'.[1] Their enthusiasm was infectious. The asceticism of their lives and their courage in witnessing to passengers and staff was impressive. This was all new to me.

One of the most deeply moving wedding ceremonies I ever officiated at was that of two members of the Children of God. They were about to set off to South America on a missionary journey. What it lacked in dignity and decorum it made up for in a deep happy faith full of expectancy. Yes, God was going to do great things! Again it was the music I found most moving. I tape-recorded the ceremony and when I listen to it now, over ten years later, I am still buoyed up by the youthful enthusiasm of a very happy occasion. The wedding reception was in the back garden. Everyone seemed to bring some 'goodies'. It was a 'common pot' and even curious bystanders were invited to join in the celebration. Religion came easily to these youngsters and yet already they were entertaining gnawing doubts about the Church. These doubts would ultimately result in a complete rupture. 'The Church lacks life and vitality' they said. Some eventually found their way back to the Church, others strayed into a non-denominational Christianity. It was several years before I began to evaluate seriously the phenomenon of the burgeoning religious groups scattered throughout the city and country.

In the early seventies Ireland was traumatised by the events in Northern Ireland. Our country became the focus for itinerant preachers, healers and prophets from abroad, mostly from America. My position as chaplain in the airport meant that I was often their first point of contact. On one occasion I received a telephone call from the main terminal building. The owner of the southern states drawl at the other end of the phone explained how he had received a prophecy in relation to the Northern problem. He wondered whether I could have his prophecies published in the Irish daily newspapers.

'Jews for Jesus', an American group of convert Jews, arrived and immediately headed for Belfast. They felt they had a special call to pray and fast for peace in Ireland.

On one occasion a box of audio tapes arrived at my home with instructions to retain them until the evangelical charismatic preacher could come to Ireland to supervise their distribution and arrange speaking engagements.

Making News

Anyone who has been reading the Irish newspapers for the past decade is aware of a general concern about many of the new religious groups. Terms like 'de-programming', 'brainwashing', 'born again', 'indoctrination', 'cult', 'love bombing' and 'being saved' have become part of our standard vocabulary.

Most people were unaware of the existence of the new and more bizarre religious groups until the Mary Canning story broke. In September 1981 *The Sunday Press* reported that 'Irish demonstrators from San Francisco, seeking the return of the Donegal girl Mary Canning from the Moonies sect, yesterday fought a pitched battle with members of the cult at the Moonies' ranch outside San Francisco where Mary is being held'. For several days all the national papers in Ireland were full of the story. Incidentally it was an event with a happy ending for Mary. *The Irish Press* recorded the story this way: 'Dublin journalists have seldom seen a more universal press conference than that in which Mary Canning, the ex-Moonie, featured yesterday. The "deprogrammed" Donegal girl sat in the Seanad Éireann anteroom and renounced the Moonies, flanked by her family and American psychologist Allen Tate-Wood, a former member of the same sect'. On that occasion it was a case of 'all's well that ends well'.

Considerable controversy was generated by the 'Ballaghaderreen scandal'. In 1981 a group of young people formally left the Roman Catholic Church to establish their non-denominational Christian fellowship. This new group styled itself the Ballaghaderreen Christian Prayer Fellowship. The group, according to its leader at the time, 'based their beliefs principally on scriptural readings and on direct appeal to God'. They admitted that this involved 'rejecting the sacraments and the entire "mediation" system of the Church as irrelevant'.[2] It was claimed that 'The group have carried out their own baptismal rites of total immersion in the waters of nearby Lough Gara. This latter rite led to an unsuccessful approach by Jehovah's Witness leaders because of the similarity of their own baptismal rites'.[3]

Another incident in 1983 involved the Elim Pentecostal

Church. Liam and Ann Kennedy alleged that their daughter Emer who had been working in Ballinasloe was abducted. They said that when she became a 'born again Christian' she 'changed from a happy normal girl to a totally different person'. A concerned group of people from Charlestown, Emer's home town, picketed a religious bookshop run by the Elim Pentecostals in Athlone in an attempt to seek redress. They were not successful.

The ongoing contentiousness generated by the activities of hitherto unknown groups is illustrated by an incident involving the Hare Krishna. In October 1982 in the High Court in Dublin a member of the Hare Krishna told the court that her four year old baby had been abducted from her mobile home at the movement's headquarters. This had happened because she had intended marrying another member of the Hare Krishna after only a few months acquaintance. Both sets of parents objected and sought custody of her child from a previous marriage. One newspaper, in familiar journalese, carried a banner headline: 'Tug-of-Love Child Handed Over to her Mother'.

A bewildering number of new groups have received significant media attention in the past few years. Transcendental Meditation (TM), for one, has been accused by its antagonists of being an eastern religion that produces arrogance and self-centredness. Supporters of TM, on the other hand, claim it is strictly secular and 'sells itself chiefly as an aid to better health and the development of one's potential'.[4]

A Late Late Show in 1982 had as one of its principal guests a Michael Cox who claimed he was Father Superior of the Irish Orthodox Catholic and Apostolic Church, an order he founded himself and which conducts services in his Dublin home.

An unusual group entitled 'The Astro-Soul Movement' managed to get itself a quarter of a page in *The Cork Examiner* of 19 January 1983. A spokesperson for the group, Dr Bettina Lowman, claimed that the movement was not a religion, 'it is more a way of life'. She said the movement 'is for people who are sincerely searching for the answers to the mysteries of their lives'.

The Way International, a spurious mixture of pseudo-scholarship and ultra-fundamentalist scripture, was described as 'one of the most sinister cults operating in Ireland'[5] by one well-known columnist in a Dublin evening paper.

A group that advertised extensively in a prestigious Dublin daily, 'The School of Philosophy and Economic Science' was bitterly condemned by an Anglican Bishop as an insidious organisation that was 'ruining people's lives'.[6]

Evangelical Christian groups like Bill Bright's 'Campus Crusade for Christ' and the 'Full Gospel Businessmen's Fellowship' have all received varying degrees of publicity.

An interesting radio interview with four Protestant ministers took place on the BBC's Sunday Sequence in May 1983. One Pentecostal minister claimed that '50 per cent of our workers in the South are converted Roman Catholics. We see ourselves in a missionary situation'. He went on to describe how 'our work is carried out through open-air witness, door-to-door visitation, tract distribution, book sales, and film shows'. The Pentecostal minister further commented that 'when we look on the south of Ireland we see a field of evangelism we want to get involved in. We don't go down there seeing Protestants or Catholics, we go down seeing sinners who need to be saved'.

Another clergyman confirmed that the south was indeed mission territory. On the same radio programme the Rev. Alan Mitchell said that 'the news had spread around the world that there was a stirring in the Roman Catholic Church in the South, there was a renewal, an awakening. We have seen many groups arrive at Dublin Airport, all trying to corner out a share of the market'. Ireland has become mission territory for evangelical non-denominational Christian groups and for religious and quasi-religious groups with an Eastern background.

It is now over ten years since my introduction to the Divine Light Mission. The encounter simply whetted my appetite to know more about the powerful dynamic that seemed to be generated within so many esoteric religious groups today.

The International Scene
The mind-boggling *cause célèbre* that focused world-wide public attention on the extraordinary nature of the new fringe religious groups was the mass suicide of more than nine hundred people at

Jonestown, Guyana. Jim Jones, who perished with his People's Temple Colony, came from dreary poverty in an industrial backwater of Indiana. He became a faith healer who eventually built a theocratic dictatorship that used religion to camouflage a bitter class hatred and a serious flirtation with Marxism. It was claimed that at one point he had 20,000 followers. He had gained considerable political influence in San Francisco before the fatal move to Guyana.

On 18 November 1979 in Jonestown, a ramshackle settlement hacked out of the jungle, 910 people willingly committed suicide. They queued up to sip a poisonous mixture at Jones' invitation. He told them they were dying with dignity for God's sake. What strange power did Jones possess that he was able to manipulate so many people? *The Wall Street Journal* went back to the fourteenth century to find a parallel. It made the comment that 'The appeal of the cults expresses the profoundness of the human will to believe, the longing for the certainty of faith'.

Five years after the horrific mass suicides of the People's Temple new religious groups continue to proliferate. It has been suggested that 'the number and variety of today's cults may be without historic precedent'. One of the largest groups, that of Rev. Sun Myung Moon's Unification Church, claims a following of 2.8 million people in 138 countries, more than 2 million of whom joined after Jonestown. According to *US News and World Report* an estimated 30 million Americans, many of whom are already members of established religions, have participated in 'offbeat' spiritual activities that range from studying horoscopes to worshipping the devil. Again, according to Gallup, 'twenty per cent of Americans believe in Astrology. Four per cent of those polled were adherents of Transcendental Meditation, three per cent practised Yoga, two per cent were charismatic Christians, two per cent followed some kind of mysticism and one per cent belonged to Eastern religions'. So-called cults and sects make news and therefore the media worldwide is inclined to inflate the importance and influence of these new groups. Others have tended to attribute devilish evil to every new group that positions itself outside the mainstream of acceptable religious orthodoxy.

Concern about the activities of religious and quasi-religious groups has attracted the attention of the European Paliament. A report was presented to the Youth Commission of the Parliament by a member from the United Kingdom, Richard Cottrell. The report warned strongly of the dangers arising from the ever-increasing numbers of sects, especially in the US and Europe. The two year investigation that preceded the debate by the Parliament identified 600 cults in the European Community. The proposals before the Parliament include guaranteed access to members of cults by their families and friends at all times and the open identification of religious movements. Cult members were said 'to be lobbying furiously in Brussels and Strasbourg against the adoption of proposed voluntary guidelines which are expected to find favour with the Parliament'.[8]

In 1980 it was reported that in France a parliamentary 'Mission d'Information sur les Sects' was exploring the legal aspects of the cult phenomenon.

In West Germany, the national minister for youth, family and health issued a new report on cults. It summarised the growth and activities of the better-known groups, giving details on recruitment techniques and the manner in which members are effectively isolated from their environment. The types of legal action which may be taken are listed, and suggestions for the protection and support of those affected are given in the document which provides funding for research on the cult problem in Germany.[8]

In Ireland secularisation has been less evident than elsewhere in the western world. New religious groups have also been less evident. However, there is no room for complacency when we consider the size of our young population and reflect on the fact that proportionally the greatest percentage of church-goers are in the middle age-group. Young people are now looking for alternatives. Some already find that new religious groups provide spiritual fulfilment, a direction and vision for their lives and a form of community that the main-line historic churches are unable to meet.

The word cult is a pejorative term of disapproval or even of abuse. *The Oxford Dictionary* defines cult as 'a system of religious worship or ritual; a group of believers'. One person I spoke to explained the difficulties involved in using this word. He said, 'in Belfast Pentecostalism would be considered a valid church, while in Sligo it would be seen by many people as a cult'. I am not going to enter into this controversy. Where possible I will use the term 'new religious group' or simply 'religious' or 'quasi-religious group'. The terms 'cult' and 'sect' have been used far too loosely to denigrate, often without cause, perfectly legitimate religious beliefs and practices.

NOTES

1. See pp. 83-85, *infra.*
2. *The Irish Press,* 8 October 1981.
3. *The Sunday Tribune,* 11 October 1981.
4. T.M. — The Other Side, *The Sunday Press,* 28 October 1981.
5. The *Evening Herald,* 9 October 1981.
6. *The Irish Press,* 9 October 1981.
7. *The Guardian,* 7 February 1984.
8. News and Views — Deo Gloria Outreach, September 1980, p. 2.

2

THE "BORN AGAIN" CHRISTIAN GROUPS

Who Are They?

Media attention has tended to focus on the apparently more bizarre groups like the Moonies, the Hare Krishna and the Divine Light Mission. In fact, over the past fifteen years the revivalist groups have been the most numerous newcomers to Ireland. Most of these 'born again' Christian groups share a common American origin, namely Campus Crusade for Christ, Teen Challenge, Greater Europe Mission, World Vision, the Full Gospel Businessmen's Fellowship, the Church of Christ, Prison Fellowship. Other evangelical Christian groups like Youth with a Mission and the Hospital Christian Fellowship do not claim American inspiration. Some common features are immediately obvious in these groups. The members tend to be intelligent, outgoing, charismatic, caring and a little boastful.

Other new groups with American origins make no effort to conceal a vitriolic anti-Catholicism. The Lifegate Bible Baptist Church and Chick Publications outdo one another in vilifying the Church. A milder example of the poison they preach will illustrate their stance. One Chick pamphlet asks 'Are Roman Catholics Christians?' It answers the question like this- 'No, not in any sense of the word. They are very religious and they are very lost. Slaves of the whore of Revelations'. The Lifegate Bible Baptist Church, publishing from an address in Templeogue, Dublin, claims that it can 'show that almost every doctrine or tradition of the Roman Catholic Church goes either contrary to or is not found in scripture'.

While the 'born again' Christian groups continue to attract Irish converts in increasing members the leadership and inspiration is often provided from outside the country. Even where the leadership is Irish a system of spiritual discipleship from abroad ensures that the groups seldom take on an indigenous spiritual dimension.

Some of the new groups do not belong to a 'born again' Christian organisation or church. Rather they share in a growing 'house church' movement that participates in a form of shepherding or pastoring which often receives its direction from well-known American evangelists.

Who Joins and Why?

The bulk of the recruits to the new evangelical groups come from disaffected members of the main-line Christian denominations. Numerous young people see the Churches as being unable to provide them with genuine spiritual experience and they are impatient with the inability of the Churches to harness the essential goodness and goodwill of many of their members.

One young Catholic girl deeply involved with a non-denominational evangelical group claimed in the course of a letter to me: 'I am in fellowship with people from evangelical groups and they are so alive with the Lord! Even though I have decided to remain in the Catholic Church I am a Catholic in name only. My sympathy, my identity and my leadership comes from non-Catholic groups. I don't think a lot of the Catholic Church.'

A concerned parent confirmed the view that the Church's presentation of the gospel does not have the same appeal or impact as that of the evangelical groups. 'As a parent whose older children have left the Catholic Church for other Christian groups I would agree that the traditional presentation of our Christianity does not meet the spiritual needs of our youth', she wrote to me. I cannot resist quoting her postscript: 'when I wrote to the Church authorities I got a courteous reply suggesting that I raise the matter with our parish priest. That good man was seventy-five years of age and with the best will in the world, unable to assist!'

Fr Jack Finnegan, writing in *The Furrow,* pointed out that 'secession points to the fact that some groups — for now or for always — have lost hope in the Church's ability to offer an acceptable framework for life and worship.'[1] His assessment of the Irish situation is particularly apt from my own experience —'where teaching is sought and needed but not forthcoming, then others listening to different music will come in and sing a different song. Then error will be allowed to stand in place of truth.'

There is a deep desire in many young hearts to know the Lord. The basic goodness of their lives is evidenced by their concern for the deprived and for the third world issues of poverty, justice and peace. The essential goodwill towards the Church is often manifested by a continuing respect for clergy and religious. However, the point of alienation arrives through the Church's inability to deliver with power the message of the gospel of salvation. Evangelisation today, that is bringing young people into a personal relationship with Jesus Christ, is often hindered in the Church not through the laziness of Christians but through the busyness of Christians in the wrong area. There is disillusionment with the presentation of what ought to be at heart a very exciting message. On the other hand there is conviction, power and an effective pastoral strategy among many of the new evangelical groups that have recently arrived in Ireland. I am surprised that they have not managed to attract more disaffected young people.

Searching Youth

Young people today are occasionally caricatured as irresponsible and funloving. Some, I'm sure are. However a feature of those attracted to evangelical groups is their sincere searching for a deeper meaning to life.

Extracts from testimonies published in an evangelical magazine provide a partial illustration of this.

> 'Rather than live in dark despair I choose to trust myself to Christ on the basis "he loved me and died for me"' - John.
>
> 'I used to sit in a bar and think of the meaning of life. All I wanted to know was why — what — where was I bound for' — Simon.

'I could see no more reason for living without God and yet I could find no convincing argument for the existence of God. Nobody could answer my questions to my satisfaction' - Patricia.

'I'm real sad that I need to commit my life to Him before I could experience the joy of having Him as my personal friend' — Mary.

'I had reached a low in my life. I called out to Christ' —Seán.

Many leave the Church in time of spiritual need. They may fail to find spiritual nourishment in the Roman Catholic Church and decide to look elsewhere. In the US a study revealed that 29 per cent of those who left the Church at a time of spiritual need were subsequently associated with Baptist, Pentecostal, or Mormon Churches. The study commented that 'others are ripe for out-conversion, since their predispositions for change are strong. When facilitating persons appear they will join other groups'.[2]

A few years ago, together with some friends, I signed up for a course in evangelisation. The course was given by an evangelical group. There was much in the content of the course that we found very difficult to accept doctrinally. However, on completion of our training we were invited to do some 'field work'.

We were sent in pairs into the centre of Dublin city to share our faith, using the techniques we had been taught. Some went to Heuston Station, the Dandelion Market, McDonalds, Trinity College campus and elsewhere. After a few hours evangelising we re-assembled to evaluate our experience. We found, almost without exception, that people wanted to listen. There was a hunger for God. There was a genuine searching for answers to the deepest problems of life. I was honestly surprised at the positive reaction.

Dean Hoge, in his study of religious change among Catholics, quotes the story of Ron, a former Catholic, and summarises his spiritual odyssey like this: 'Ron felt a strong spiritual need at the time he was answering the call of the Lord during college, and he sought out religious counsel from several priests, ministers, professors. His spiritual quest was guided by his reaction to these leaders. He did not find Fr Leonard helpful, since he was too intellectual. But he did respond to TAG (a Pentecostal fellowship) since "the spirit of God flows in that place", and he immediately followed the Reverend Durham; in Ron's words, "Boom, when I went in there, I knew it". His period of seekership had ended for a time, since he is about to marry a girl who is committed to the New Prophecy Church, as he is, and this will strengthen his ties there'.[3] The story of Ron is the story of an increasing number of young Catholic boys and girls in Ireland.

In regard to the seeker type of person who opts out of the Church to join another religious group it is worth quoting from *Lapsing Children: A Sociologist's Comment.* 'The seeker-rebel rejects her parents and also their religious practice and values while retaining some religious belief. This type may often turn to the New Religious Movements to express their belief and to provide them with an alternative set of moral guidelines. In many cases they may have gone through a dropout phase or experiment with drugs, sex, petty larceny as a part of their rejection of their parents and materialistic values.'[4]

Fellowship

Catholics can feel isolated in living out their faith. Dr Dean Hoge says that 'the finding of our study was that personal relationships are more important than doctrine in general. I'm not talking about gimmicky things, but real, authentic personal relationships, with people sharing where they are in life and supporting each other. That is the most important thing when it comes to bringing people into a Church or losing them'.[5] The evangelical groups working in Ireland are small and tightly knit. Many of them can programme activities like Bible study, child care, study weekends, outreach apostolates that get their members involved with each other. In contrast, Catholic parishes can seem cold and impersonal. For those who are drawn to the spiritual life there grows a desire for a life lived at a more intense level. This was confirmed to me by Seán, an ex-Roman Catholic who joined an evangelical group: 'I received a good sense of direction from the group. The Church is too diffuse; in the group there is a much more intense life'. Nick Cavnar, writing in *New Covenant* magazine, endorsed this view: 'Catholics who have experienced an evangelical spirituality can feel particularly isolated within their parishes, where few people share their style of prayer or their enthusiasm'.[6] 'Sometimes we feel so drawn to the Assembly of God churches', one couple wrote. 'We are welcomed there and can join in their praise session and feel so uplifted — something we never experience in our own Church'.

After initial contact with the group a potential convert often stays because of the genuine love and fellowship. In the beginning, Catholics will lead a parallel spiritual life; sacramental in the Church and purely biblical within the group.

Eventually a choice must be made. One person I interviewed reluctantly agreed that 'the group encouraged me to leave the Church'.

It's a crazy world of confusion where so many personal relationships are based on selfishness. Other relationships are functional, 'let's get together to do this or that'. It's a beautiful surprise for young people to find themselves in a group where there is caring and concern. Because of the rudimentary knowledge many Catholics have of their religion, weaning them away from 'unscriptural practices' isn't too difficult.

Evangelical Spirituality

Evangelical spirituality has an immediacy that is exciting and attractive to young people. God is acting forcefully in the 'here and now'. Miracles and healings are happening. God is praised in every situation. The hymns, all simple, with tuneful melodies, emphasise God's love, power and goodness. The same phrases are often repeated over and over again, 'God is good, God is good. Now I am free, now I am free, God is good. He took away my sins'.

Personal testimony is an important feature of evangelical spirituality. It often begins with a person recalling how they had been invited to, or stumbled upon a prayer meeting. Episodes of their past sinful life are related. The conversion experience, usually instantaneous and dramatic, is told in detail. Life is changed. No more problems. As one man said to me 'He is beside me. He fills all the empty gaps in my life'.

A feature of evangelical worship is the opportunity given to all to participate. The neophyte and the mature Christian, men and women, are all listened to with equal respect and attention.

In terms of teaching the emphasis is much more on gift than learning. This of course means that ministry is not something confined to a particular person or class. Spiritual ministry is open to all.

There is no embarrassment in sharing spiritual topics, often of a very personal nature, both inside and outside of actual worship. Quite the contrary. God is spoken of in terms of great familiarity. His activity is seen in even the smallest detail of family and social life.

There are many elements in evangelical spirituality that attract young people. It is in stark contrast with the anonymity and ritualistic nature of main-line Christian worship. It is much more a shared spirituality, non-clerically dominated and certainly more personally exciting.

What being 'Born Again' means

Because Irish Catholics have grown up in a homogeneous religious environment they feel threatened by the unknown. The vocabulary of Irish Catholic spirituality has been hallowed by a long tradition. We have dressed up the message of Jesus in a technical, sacramental, theological language. Phrases like 'the blood of the lamb', or 'claiming the victory', or indeed 'standing on the blood of Jesus', are virtually incomprehensible to the average Irish Roman Catholic. A pamphlet I have in my possession at the moment brashly proclaims 'no confessional but the throne of grace'. This is published by an evangelical group recently established here. The vocabulary of the Protestant evangelical tradition can be a real barrier to understanding the spiritual realities behind it.

I was very surprised to be asked by a casual acquaintance I met at a prayer meeting whether I had been 'saved' or not. I was nonplussed. I replied with a certain degree of confusion that 'being saved' was part of a process that I was undergoing at the moment. 'I was saved five years ago', my friend volunteered enthusiastically. 'Yes, I accepted Jesus as my Lord and Saviour one Friday night', he continued. My Roman Catholic upbringing, and even my seminary training has not equipped me to cope with concepts like this. At that time, and perhaps even today, very few Roman Catholics would understand the evangelical Protestant when he talks about 'being saved' or 'being born again'. However the term has become more familiar in recent years thanks to the media reports on a significant number of conversions among para-military prisoners in Northern Ireland. Almost all of the conversions that we have heard about seem to have been of the 'born again' variety. A number of para-militaries have actually surrendered themselves to the security forces because of their conversion experiences. The most notable of these is Kevin McGrady from Belfast's Markets area, the Provo who returned from Amsterdam to confess to a murder for which he is now serving a life sentence after 'seeing the light'.[7]

To 'be saved' is to accept Jesus Christ as Saviour and Lord. One's sins are forgiven and cancelled through this act of faith; Jesus comes into one's heart and a new life begins. This is also called being 'born again'. It means to have a life-changing experience. The scriptural justification for the term comes from the Gospel of St John, 'truly, truly, I say to you, unless one is born anew, he cannot see the Kingdom of God'. *(Jn 3:3)*

The process of initiation in the Protestant evangelical tradition can best be explained thus:

1. You must believe and accept all that Jesus taught.

2. You must profess your faith in these beliefs.

3. You must depart from your past sinful ways by receiving the Father's new life, which makes you a 'born again' Christian.

Many groups operating in Ireland today would class themselves as 'born again' Christians, or simply as Christians. A number of these claim that they alone are Christians. A feature of the 'saved' or 'born again' Christian is an elitist attitude towards other Christians who do not claim the 'born again' tag. There is generally a critical attitude on the part of 'born again' Christians towards the main-line historical Christian Churches.

Having a 'born again' experience does not initiate one into any particular denomination. Nor does it necessarily have any connection with the Sacrament of Baptism. An acquaintance of mine, Jim Walsh, of the Greater Europe Mission, a non-denominational mission working in the north Dublin suburbs, confirmed this for me. He wrote, 'as evangelical Christians we do believe all people everywhere, regardless of Church affiliation, need to be born again to see the Kingdom of God. We do not see the new birth spoken of by Jesus as synonymous with baptism'. A few evangelical groups will deny the necessity of baptism altogether. Others would claim that only adult baptism has any spiritual efficacy. There are also those who say that only adult baptism and baptism by immersion are scriptural.

My experience is that almost all 'born again' Christians would consider the run-of-the-mill Roman Catholic as 'not saved'. In Ireland very few evangelicals would be prepared to admit this publicly nor would the majority preach it. Many would believe that if a Roman Catholic has a 'born again' experience the genuineness of the experience ought to be demonstrated by his leaving the Roman Catholic Church. I know many Roman Catholics who have been asked, 'how can you possibly be born again and remain a Catholic?' To confirm this viewpoint I would like to quote from a Protestant evangelical source. 'If a Roman Catholic claims to have come into an experience through which they claim to be in a personal relationship with Jesus Christ through the experience of the "Baptism of the Spirit" then their salvation must be the same as ours. If this is so why do they remain inside the Roman Catholic Church? Why do they persist in practising the Roman Catholic religion? One of the most inconsistent and unscriptural things today is to be "an evangelical Roman Catholic".'[8]

The 'Born Again' Christian and the Bible

The 'born again' Christian generally tends to be a fundamentalist when it comes to interpreting scripture. The first principle of the Protestant fundamentalist is that the Bible is the sole and authoritative source of any doctrine's authenticity. Most evangelical fundamentalist groups would interpret the Bible literally down to the last dot and comma.

Controversy concerning the interpretation of scripture has been around for a long time. In March 1925 the state legislature of Tennessee in America passed legislation deeming it unlawful to teach anything but the literal interpretations of scripture in any of the state schools. The American Civil Liberties Group decided to test the constitutionality of this legislation. This resulted in the so-called 'monkey trial', later made into an Academy Award winning film. John Scopes, a biology teacher, was found guilty of teaching the theory of evolution in the Dayton High School. The prosecution case, backed by the World Fundamentalist Association, relied heavily on the literal interpretation of the creation story in the book of Genesis to win its case. Scopes was fined $100 and costs on 24 July 1925. Fundamentalists today still fight the teaching of evolution in public schools and elsewhere.

The term 'fundamentalist' is used to describe a religious movement that started in America in 1909 among various Protestant denominations. One of the movement's objectives was to maintain the traditional and literal interpretation of scripture. Fundamentalists claim that the Bible has been verbally inspired by the Holy Spirit, almost by dictation, and therefore anyone who can read can understand it. It is said of fundamentalists that they cannot speak of their history, their present, or their future in isolation from God who makes all things happen. 'Bad things happen as God's chastisement of us or as God's way of closing doors on mere human plans. Good things are blessings from God. God is always good but his goodness is sometimes rather terrible'.[9] Fundamentalists make little scholarly effort to determine the meaning the biblical writers intended in their own times. They simply interpret the scriptures according to the literal meaning of the words in the vernacular of the day.

A problem with many Protestant evangelical groups is that individuals interpret scripture according to the meaning each takes out of the words. This practice of individual interpretation of scripture has contributed to the breakdown of Protestantism into a profusion of churches and fellowships. One of the most extraordinary sights in Africa, in Nigeria, particularly, is to see a sign at every cross roads pointing to a different 'aladura' Church.

Despite protestations to the contrary, the exclusively biblical approach to revelation and divine truth gradually undermines faith in the Church. A friend of mine belonged to one well-known evangelical group that stressed their attempts to build up people within their own Churches. She wrote to me as follows: 'After about nine months with the group I began to feel more and more anti-Church vibrations. Even though many of the staff and young people talked of the great need for the Church, the obvious negative feelings towards it and particularly towards the Catholic Church came across strongly. Very frequently I heard that "many priests are not saved". It is true that the Irish Catholic Church and many priests in it are in need of repair but it is unfair to speak out so strongly if one is not prepared to help build it up.'

The House Church Movement

Apart from the more evangelical Christian groups a new phenomenon has appeared on the Irish scene. I am speaking of the house church. A 'house church' is a group of Christians who come together in private houses, under a pastoral head, for prayer, worship and breaking of bread or 'the Lord's Supper'. Members and adherents who have felt rejected by their own churches have found refuge in the house churches.

There is a sincere attempt to model the house church on early New Testament Christianity. They say, 'let's get away from the outmoded and corrupt historical Christian Churches, and base our life on how the early Christians lived'. One ex-Roman Catholic, Tony, described it to me in the following fashion. 'In the past I was a person who never missed Mass, I went the whole hog on all the religious trimmings. Then I was captured with the idea of just being a Christian — the type of Christian one reads about in the scriptures. I was attracted to the notion of taking my instructions from the Lord and from him alone. In that way I had got to be right. I began to see that things like the Mass and confession were not needed. I found I could pray to God and seek information from him. I didn't find confession compatible with scripture.'

Within the 'house church' phenomenon there are certain common characteristics. They claim not to be a new denomination — indeed, some within the house church Movement argue that it is the one true Church. The Methodist Church Mission Report[10] published in 1984 said of the house church movement that 'it may reasonably be described as a sect on the way to becoming a denomination. Some within the house church are willing to cooperate freely with the historic Church; others remain aloof.' The same Methodist Report, while praising the House Church's emphasis on clear teaching, joyous worship, and pastoral care said that 'the way in which members of other Churches are proselytised is to be regretted.' It also makes the criticism that 'nowhere in scripture has a member to ask permission of others to change house or job or to marry, but in some areas of the House Church this very legalistic practice is certainly the case.'

The growth of the house church movement has been a matter of serious concern to many Christian Churches in Britain. The same is true in Northern Ireland where a particularly robust controversy was carried on in the newspapers early in 1983. In Dublin, this movement of non-denominational independent Christian Churches has grown steadily, to the point where about twelve of them now exist. In the south of Ireland, disillusioned Catholics form the bulk of the membership. However, these groups are also siphoning off the membership of some of the Protestant Churches.

In most cases the leadership of the house church movement is provided by untrained and theologically naïve lay people. There can be a real danger that some of the groups of people will be misled, particularly through the imprudent use of the ministries of exorcism and healing.

At a point in people's lives they need to hear the clear gospel. Quite often the people who drift into a house church claim that they are not hearing the basic, fundamental gospel proclaimed in the Catholic Church. Fr Alvin Illig, the Executive Director of the Committee on Evangelisation for the National Conference of Catholic Bishops in the United States says 'research has indicated that bad preaching is one of the major reasons for disedification with the Catholic Church. In this ecumenical age people don't think anything at all of going down the street to hear some powerful preaching at the Pentecostal Church. As our Protestant brothers put it, the sheep will be fed by whomsoever feeds them. If we fail to feed our people, they're going to go looking some place else.'

In the course of researching the material for this book I have interviewed many lapsed Catholics and the deep sadness is that I hear a common complaint: 'I wasn't being fed spiritually in the Church.' Often those who leave are truly zealous and prayerful people who love God and sincerely want to follow him. Very few leave for theological reasons. The theological reasons come much later. They hear a message preached with power. They experience a fellowship or community. They receive regular pastoral care. All this is new. To return to the Church would be like leaving a warm fireside to head out into a winter's night. In honesty I have to witness to the edification I have received from evangelical Protestant brothers and sisters. The quality of many of their Christian lives is truly a light shining in the darkness. They are generous with time, money, hospitality and love. Many of them belong to house churches.

The House Church Movement depends very much on the personal pastoral qualities of the leaders. Where there are strong Christian men in positions of leadership the House Church thrives. Where this not the case it may continually divide or even die away. The personality of the leader is often indispensable if a House Church is to survive.

The House Church Movement, rather than fostering the unity for which Jesus prayed, further divides the body of Christ. It sees itself as a twentieth century expression of the only apostolic Church. But history cannot be ignored. The ideal Church exists only in heaven. Peter found it difficult to work harmoniously with Paul. Paul and Barnabas separated in their missionary apostolates because of basic personality differences. Some early Christians had scruples about eating certain foods, while others did not, and so on. The early Church had to learn how to cope with the differences while maintaining the essential unity of the Church. Forming one's own ideal Church is hardly a solution to difficult Church problems.

The House Church ignores the 2,000 years of Church history. The basic message of the gospels is clear. However, over the years the Church has had to confront a bewildering number of issues and problems. It was to meet the pastoral needs of the Christian people that the Church developed a body of teaching that would help clarify, interpret and apply the truths found in the Bible and in the faith of the early Christian community. Different heresies arose to challenge particular points of doctrine or the Bible's teaching. To meet these challenges the bishops of the Church formulated a body of teaching over the years to preserve the unity and truth of the Christian message. Church laws also helped believers to apply scriptural principles to their daily lives. For example, the obligation to attend Mass once a week is based on scripture (Acts 2:46-7, Heb 10:25) and on the many other Christian writings that consider worship together on the Lord's day an essential part of Christian life. Jesus also said to the apostles 'He who hears you hears me, and he who rejects you rejects me' (Lk 10:16.) He gave authority to Church leaders to teach. That was his command. A Roman Catholic believes that the Church teaches with the authority that Jesus gave to the apostles. Fr Jack Finnegan, writing in *The Furrow*, claims that what began as a laudable desire for renewal, by a subtle monopoly of the Holy Spirit, loses a sense of history and tradition, refuses to recognise authority or submit to objective discernment and begins a process that results in a break with the Church.[11]

There is a hunger for God abroad. Jim Walsh, of the Greater Europe Mission wrote to me: 'As I'm sure you yourself are aware, people in Ireland today are desperately seeking a more meaningful relationship with God through a personal relationship with Jesus Christ. Because this is so, the Fellowship Bible Church is blooming with new faces. Most of these people have come of their own accord as total strangers. One has come bringing another. They have come seeking spiritual help. Last month a class for new Christians was started in the Fellowship Bible House Church to provide answers from the Bible to the questions these new Christians are asking'.

In the past twenty years Catholics have got used to people leaving the Church because of birth control or priestly celibacy or the changes in the Mass. No one knows quite how to respond to people who say they are leaving because they have found Jesus. And yet this is increasingly becoming a fact. Catholics with an inadequate grasp of their own Church heritage are particularly vulnerable to the subtle attacks on Catholic teaching which are made by some fundamentalist Protestants.

The answer to the 'come out-ism' encouraged by the House Church Movement is a more effective form of pastoral care combined with solid scriptural teaching, proclaimed with conviction. I believe this movement has not reached its peak. It will continue to attract young, disgruntled Roman Catholics in increasing numbers.

Evangelical Christian Groups and Recruitment

As someone who has been involved in the Charismatic Renewal Movement for over ten years I have been positioned better than most to witness the methods of recruitment of evangelical groups. Unfortunately, some of those who have left the Church have come from within the ranks of this movement.

When a person becomes involved in the Charismatic Renewal Movement and experiences the phenomenon known as the Baptism in the Spirit, they become spiritually sensitive. Many develop a deep and genuine spirituality. Sone of this has been built on Pentecostal spirituality fed by fundamentalist literature. I have found books like *The Cross and the Switchblade* by David Wilkinson, and *Prison to Praise* by Merlin Crothers, helpful. But a diet of these books supplemented by audio tapes recorded by Pentecostal preachers can corrode a faith that has no theological foundation. Teaching that relies heavily on a particularly narrow and literal interpretation of scripture unsupported by Church tradition gives a distorted emphasis to the message of God's word. Prayer meetings of the Charismatic Renewal have attracted evangelical Christians as a launching pad for their Irish missionary endeavours. They have been welcomed. They have frequently been invited to teach, occasionally even to participate in the pastoral care of a particular group. Uninformed Roman Catholics have been convinced by superspiritual language, by an apparently deep knowledge of scripture and by a genuine caring attitude, to abandon the faith they have been brought up in.

Christian Rock Music

A strategy that is being increasingly used by evangelical non-denominational Christians for the purposes of evangelisation is Christian rock music. Groups such as Living Sound, The Celebration Singers, The Forerunners, The Blood of the Lamb and others, all American, have arrived and offered their services in Ireland; their methods included the use of 'altar calls', that is, calling people forth to accept Jesus into their lives at the end of the concert.

The danger here is emotional manipulation and the lack of a pastoral back-up to support the commitments that have been made.

Similarly, summer camps or Bible schools for children have attracted many participants.

Tract Distribution

The ministry of the Word through the distribution of tracts, tapes, books and educational aids is another method used by non-denominational Christian groups in Ireland. One ex-Catholic told me that he had distributed 100,000 pieces of literature since returning to Ireland in 1970. Evangelical literature from America, some of it of the 'hate' variety, is now being widely distributed. A ship called 'Logos' has visited Dublin port solely for the purpose of displaying and selling evangelical Protestant literature. On a recent visit to Dublin it carried no item of Catholic spiritual literature. It is difficult to reconcile these facts with the claims of many non-denominational Christian groups that their aim is spiritual renewal within the existing Christian denominations.

False Ecumenism

One of the reasons why evangelical groups succeed in attracting Catholics is the prevalence of a confused and woolly ecumenism. Ecumenical activity is often seen as an attempt, primarily and solely, to acknowledge those matters of faith which the different Christian Churches hold in common. Expressions of denominational positions either in speech or in worship are altogether avoided. A Protestant review, *Theological Renewal* pointed out the futility of this approach: 'A unity based on experience at the expense of doctrine would be less than the unity envisaged in the New Testament and would be dangerous in the long term.'[12] Because of a genuine and deeply experienced need to seek Christian unity Catholics feel drawn to compromise on the essentials of their Catholic faith. Lethargy in regard to the ecumenical task on the part of Church leaders breeds frustration and impatience on the part of the 'pew Catholic'. This impatience, encouraged at times by evangelical Christians, leads to a decision to leave the Church altogether.

Christian unity is a priority for all Catholics. However, its starting point must be a real respect for and openness to the sincerely-held views of others. Within our own country the obstacles are not doctrinal alone. Bishop Dermot O' Mahony comments that 'a greater obstacle to Christian unity than doctrinal differences (and these are real) can be the attitudes of intolerance and prejudice — an intolerance and prejudice that can be seen within and without a particular Church.'[13]

Deception

A final method used by some isolated evangelical groups is an unfortunate tendency to deceive the gullible. For instance, I have before me a brochure entitled 'Reachout'. It carries a photograph of Pope John Paul II and a by-line 'Pope of the People'. One would conclude from a cursory glance that it was a parish newsletter. The message the brochure carries is inimical to Roman Catholicism. The publisher was an evangelical group from the city centre of Dublin. It was dropped into my letterbox recently and included an invitation to sign up for a course in Bible study.

Some evangelical literature seriously misrepresents the Roman Catholic position on the Eucharist, the priesthood and the sacraments. They claim that much of the Church's teaching is unscriptural. They will point to the promulgation dates of certain doctrines as evidence that they are man-made doctrines.

The guiding principle in response to misrepresentation is charity and a greater degree of knowledge and appreciation of our own Catholic faith.

NOTES

1. *The Furrow*, December 1981.
2. Dean Hoge, *Converts, Dropouts, Returnees* — A study of Religious change among Catholics, The Pilgrim Press New York, p. 117.
3. *Converts, Dropouts, Returnees*, p. 124.
4. Máire Nic Ghiolla Phádraig, *Lapsing Children, Doctrine and Life*, October 1982, p. 487..
5. *Converts Dropouts, Returnees*.
6. *New Covenant*, February 1983.
7. Seamus Mulligan, *The Charismatic Controversy*, An Evangelical Protestant Society Publication, p. 26.
8. Hadden and Swann, *Prime Time Preachers*, Addison Wesley Publishing Co., p. 89.
9. Methodist Church Home Mission Report, 128/1984, p. 67.
10. *The Furrow*, December 1981.
11. *Theological Renewal* No. 68, April/May 1977.
12. *New Creation*, March 1981.

3

THE BORN AGAIN CHRISTIAN AND THE CHURCH

The evangelical Christian frequently views salvation as a once-off event. An occasion of personal commitment to Jesus Christ is the moment of salvation. Some would say, 'once saved, always saved'.

'The just live by faith' was the catch-cry of Martin Luther. He set out his thesis at Easter 1517 at the beginning of a series of lectures on the Epistle to the Hebrews. 'Man is incapable of obtaining relief from any sin by his own efforts alone. In the sight of God all human virtues are sin', he taught. Faith alone justifies.

The Catholic Church also emphasises the importance of faith. However, she believes and teaches that it is through faith combined with good works, sacraments and following the teaching of the Church that we accomplish our salvation. Cardinal Suenens puts it this way: 'When Catholics speak of being saved they have much more in mind than the one moment of a person's conversion to Jesus. For the Catholic sanctification is conceived more in terms of a growth process and less in terms of a crisis moment, though crisis experiences are not absent from Catholic tradition.'[1]

In baptism we are born into the community of the Church. Through this community we receive the care, teaching and spiritual nourishment necessary to our growth into mature Christian men and women. At each stage of our spiritual development there are particular occasions of special help called sacraments. Each of these is an important 'encounter with Christ' through which we grow into an even deeper relationship with him. While the Church views baptism as the salvation event it also considers it to be the starting point in a process of salvation. In other words, salvation is looked upon as a lifelong walk during which we grow in our relationship with the Father. Our salvation begins at the moment we are baptised, but it doesn't end until we are united with the Trinity. Catholics believe that salvation ultimately depends on the grace of God — that is, his power working through us. We seek to 'work out our salvation'. The love of God and union with Christ demand from man a positive effort to acquire a more spiritual way of life. Salvation demands much more than mere belief.

The Church has also taught that the individual cannot be completely assured of his own salvation. This does not mean we are lacking in confidence. Like St Paul 'we possess our salvation in hope of sharing the glory of God' *(Rom 5:2)*. In terms of salvation the Catholic is willing to trust in the mercy, compassion and love of God at the time of particular judgement.

The Church and the Bible

Roman Catholics believe that the word of God is available through the scriptures. They also believe that God's word is passed down through the sacred tradition of the Church throughout the ages. The scriptures were conceived, nurtured and brought to birth under the inspiration of the Holy Spirit, within the womb of God's people. The Western Bishops in their Lenten Pastoral of 1983 emphasised this point in relation to the New Testament. They wrote that: 'the Gospels didn't emerge independently of the Church. They were part of her wider preaching tradition. The point to remember is that they still are. Individual texts or passages have to be understood within the unity of all scripture and the living tradition of the Church. To separate the Scriptures from the Church is to forget their origins and distort their meaning'.

To the mother is entrusted the responsibility of teaching and directing God's people in the ways of faith. So Catholics look to the Church for interpretation, authentic teaching and the practical application of God's word in scripture to their daily lives.

The key to understanding the scriptures is not a blind literal adherence to the text. One must take into account the historical and cultural context in which the Bible was written. Even to understand the colloquial nuances of biblical terms demands some knowledge of the customs, manners of speech, political systems, practices of worship and prayer and the literary forms used by the people at the time the particular book of scripture was written. Stressing the importance of this point Pope Pius XII told Catholic biblical scholars: 'You must go back, as it were, in the spirit to those remote centuries of the East. With the aid of history, archaeology, ethnology and the other sciences, you must determine accurately what modes of writing the ancient writers would likely use and in fact did use'. We must not impose on the Bible our own twentieth century viewpoint.

In agreement with other Christians, Roman Catholics believe that 'all scripture is inspired by God' *(2 Tim 3)*. This means that the primary author is God; the human author is God's instrument. Many scholars believe that biblical authors were given a special insight by God which enabled them to communicate faithfully what God wanted them to convey.

Communicating the message of the Bible is not a matter of simply transferring information. Bible teaching is a matter of information and inspiration. It is God's word, alive and active. Evangelical Christians have made impressive pastoral use of scripture. It has rightly been used to exhort, encourage, reprove and advise those under their care.

There is a thirst for God's word rather than the private opinions of the most brilliant preacher. The life of the Catholic must be a life lived in submission to God's word in the community of the Church. The Catholic's knowledge of scripture is usually perfunctory. Where knowledge is present it is often exclusively of the intellectual kind. As I have stated again and again in this book, if we fail to preach God's word with power and conviction how can we adopt a hostile attitude when our people seek such preaching elsewhere?

Some may be tempted to ask: 'does all this mean that you have to be an intellectual to read scripture?' Not at all. We can read the word of God with confidence for our private spiritual nourishment. 'Indeed, God's word is living and active, sharper than any two-edged sword ... it judges the reflections and thoughts of the heart' *(Heb 4:12)*. Where our reading of the scripture leads to a greater fidelity, to a life of love, we can be sure that it is the Lord truly speaking to us. 'Take and read', Augustine was instructed. It is well to remember that even the scholars differ in their interpretation of scripture. A practical suggestion is to use a good authorised edition of the Bible with helpful footnotes or to buy one of the widely available cheap but excellent commentaries. It is only where we are taught something, as coming from the Bible, that conflicts with the demands of charity or the teaching of the Church, that we have an obligation to seek help. Indeed, scripture reading ought ideally to be part of the family prayer life of every Catholic home.

The Church and Religious Experience

The conversion experience frequently referred to as 'being born again' nearly always involves a sensible religious experience. This spiritual phenomenon is often termed 'Baptism in the Spirit'. One Pentecostal scholar described this experience as 'that act of grace, based on the promise of Acts 1:5 (For John baptised with water, but before many days you shall be baptised with the Holy Spirit) whereby God reveals himself to the believer in a personal, direct, intimate and continuous fashion, by bringing man under the control of and into the fullness of the Holy Spirit. Through this act the believer becomes in a distinctive way, aware of the resurrected and glorified Christ in his life'.[2] In the evangelical and Pentecostal traditions there has been an emphasis on the 'mountaintop' experience.

The average Irish Catholic is baptised as a very young infant. Depending on the quality of the Christian life in the home children will receive some knowledge of God and religious practice. They will receive the sacraments of Holy Communion, Penance and Confirmation as surely as they will pass from class to class and from primary to secondary school. Faith will continually be assumed, even taken for granted. It will often be explained solely in terms of mystery, prayer in terms of duty. Fr Liam Ryan, Professor of Sociology at St Patrick's College, Maynooth, commenting on the findings of the European Values

Study Groups carried out in 1981 wrote: 'Considering the overall level of belief it is surprising to find that a very high percentage of Irish Catholics' never had a 'religious experience' or never felt that they were 'close to God'. More particularly, a large number of people do not find Sunday Mass 'a religious experience'. Fr Ryan then makes the key point that 'it is the vitality of a living religious experience which will keep people in contact with the Church.' This conclusion is borne out by a working party which summarised the pastoral implications of Máire Nic Ghiolla Phádraig's national survey. They said that 'where the Irish Church is weakest is in the basic area of "religious experience" and "prayer".' By saying we are Christians we are essentially admitting some kind of *relationship* with the Father. When our understanding of the relationship is weak our Christianity is weak. 'God has meaning only if he is the living and personal God' writes Cardinal Suenens.[3] He also says that God 'invites all of us to experience, even here below, the warmth of his love; he has made us just for that.'

Evangelical non-denominational Christians, especially the Pentecostals, have emphasised the spiritual 'highs', whereas Roman Catholicism has always tended to stress the mystery of faith. I believe it is in the area of faith and experience that the different traditions have most to offer each other.

All experience received in a religious setting is not necessarily spiritual. There is an unfortunate tendency to ascribe to God a continuing dialogue in human terms. Thus pentecostal jargon will be liberally sprinkled with 'the Lord said to me', 'the Lord laid this on my heart', 'I had a vision'. There is very little room for spiritual dryness or difficulties of faith in this approach. From the Catholic viewpoint the grace of God 'comes to us in experience at times and in ways we least expect ... yet it must be remembered that God, in the normal course of events and especially in the history of salvation, addresses the person in the human condition. Grace grows from within nature; it does *not* bypass or destroy nature'.[4]

There is always the danger of attempting to interpret what is psychic in purely spiritual terms. I have noticed, on occasion, that people can be manipulated by the use of superspiritual language or by attributing to God actions, thoughts or fantasies that have a clear human explanation. In this whole area the two thousand year history and wisdom of the Church is important. The clergy have a clear responsibility to provide *sensitive* pastoral direction and discernment in the area of religious experience.

Another difficulty encountered in evangelical spirituality is a certain seeking after religious experience. The power of an experience is unlikely to be a test of lasting holiness. 'My food is to do the will of him who sent me' *(Jn 4:34)*, is the yardstick or test. Jesus came to serve, to lay down his life. To seek spiritual experiences for their own sake can be a form of selfishness and can open one up to the work of Satan.

Having said all that, conversion and religious experiences have been very much part of Church life from earliest times.

> I spent my vacation in the country with my son, a catechumen like myself .... When the time came that I should submit my name (for Baptism), we left the country and returned to Milan. My son also decided to be reborn along with me .... So we were baptised and the anxiety of our past life fled from us... I was deeply stirred by the voices of the Church sweetly swelling in the singing of hymns and canticles!
>
> St Augustine
Confessions

> I was not conscious to myself, on my conversion, of any change, intellectual or moral, wrought in my mind ... but it was like coming into port after a rough sea.
>
> Cardinal Newman
Apologia pro Vita Sua

> I took up a book about Gerard Manley Hopkins ... He was thinking of becoming a Catholic. He was writing letters to Cardinal Newman about becoming a Catholic.
>
> All of a sudden, something began to stir within me,

Something began to push me, to prompt me. It was a movement that spoke like a voice.

'What are you waiting for', it said. 'Why are you sitting here? Why do you hesitate? You know what you ought to do ....'

Suddenly, I could bear it no longer. I put down the book, and got into my raincoat, and started down the stairs. I went out into the street. I crossed over and walked along by the gray wooden fence (toward a Catholic rectory) in the light rain.

And then everything inside me began to sing — to sing with peace, to sing with strength and to sing with conviction.

Thomas Merton
Seven Storey Mountain

Down the ages, men and women have experienced the power of God and responded. St Benedict, St Francis, St John of the Cross and many more. St Ignatius, for one, used his experience of God as a measuring stick of all his other experiences to discern the promptings of God. The Spiritual Exercises of St Ignatius of Loyola are used even today and have been endorsed by popes and bishops. These exercises are designed to culminate in a wholehearted acceptance of 'Jesus as Lord', and you can be sure that wherever genuine Christianity exists, so also does religious experience. Most priests seem conditioned to reject anything that smacks of religious experience, and unfortunately, very few priests are equipped to identify valid religious experiences. It is small wonder then that the evangelical groups can readily gain recruits.

Personal Relationship with God

There has been over-emphasis on the cerebral in our Roman Catholic religion. It is difficult, particularly for young people, to work up enthusiasm for 'a God of the intellect' alone. There is a need to feel in some way the 'love relationship' that exists between God and us. Religion is a relationship. A matter of faith, yes. But it is a question of 'head and heart'. 'Without some personal relationship with God, nothing will last for long in your religion', writes Fr Michael Paul Gallagher.[5] When the scriptures talk about knowing God, there can be no mistaking the meaning. 'To "know God" in the scriptural sense is to experience him through a personal, intimate relationship.' When St John writes 'we have come to know and believe in the love God has for us', he is speaking of a real, concrete experience of the Father's personal love. St Paul in his Epistle to the Ephesians prays that they 'may be able to grasp fully, with all the holy ones, the breadth and length and height and depth of Christ's love, and *experience* this love which surpasses all knowledge, so that you may attain the fullness of God himself'.

The challenge to the Church is to lead people into this personal relationship with God. When God is experienced as 'Abba', as loving Father, there arises a great desire to know about this God. Youngsters who are moved by the experience of God, especially his love and forgiveness, begin to read scripture, learn how to pray, and get their lives in order. The Protestant evangelicals have brought a 'thaw' to what was previously seen as a matter of the head alone. The 'heart of the problem is the human heart' is how one evangelical put it to me.

In the area of religious experience I would like to recommend Dr Dermot Lane's work *The Experience of God – An Invitation to do Theology* (Veritas, 1985). The section entitled 'Criteria for Evaluating Religious Experience' is particularly helpful for the whole discernment process.

In the Charismatic Renewal a very simple pastoral initiative called 'the Life in the Spirit Seminars' has proved to be extraordinarily effective in bringing people into a personal relationship with Christ under his grace. I have been constantly surprised at the way in which God answered the deepest needs of people's hearts to know and love him. The experience of accepting Jesus as Lord and Saviour and knowing him in a personal and individual way has happened worldwide in many Roman Catholic prayer groups. As a result of this experience Catholics have testified to a renewed sacramental life, a thirst for reading scripture, and a new understanding and appreciation of the Mass.

The Rite of Christian Initiation of Adults has not been tried in Ireland to any great extent that I am aware of. Yet it seems to offer the possibility of bringing people into a real relationship with Christ. It evangelises by offering the Word in many forms and many ways to the indifferent, the curious and the interested. It helps those who accept the Word's invitation to repent. It involves a fairly lengthy programme of growth in faith, community life, worship, prayer and active charity. It deepens the impact of the sacraments of initiation and helps the participants to live out the spiritual implications of these sacraments. Fr Declan Connolly, while studying at Fordham University, New York, wrote: 'I found my experience of sharing in the catechumenate an invigorating and worthwhile one. It is a great sign of hope for the future. It lays stress on the experience of real community. It likewise highlights and values the specific gifts of vocation of each person ... I would think that the R.C.I.A. has great potential for renewing the Church in the modern world.'

Conclusion

Evangelicals manifest a deep personal commitment to Jesus Christ. This commitment is demonstrated in a life lived for God. There is always a tendency to self-righteousness in evangelical Christianity. Other Christians who have not come into a faith-filled relationship with God in the same way are often looked down upon and the quality of their Christianity or, indeed, its authenticity, is questioned. One commentator has claimed that 'evangelicals seem more judgemental about other Christians than about themselves'. There is a deep commitment among evangelicals to evangelism. However they often act as if other Christians, particularly those belonging to the main-line historical Christian Churches, are non-believers. Catholics are often targeted for conversion, bearing out the suspicion that they are considered 'not saved'. Manipulative hard sell techniques are often used in evangelism. One could legitimately suspect the genuineness of the conversions.

A serious lacuna in the overall activity of evangelical Christians is the lack of a serious social dimension to their apostolate. They avoid many critical social, political and economic issues that demand a response. Their activities for the underprivileged occasionally have strings attached, perhaps even an expectation of conversion. Finally, they sometimes adopt a siege mentality that identifies their fellow Christian as their foe. It is sometimes simpler to know who and what they are against than what they are for.

We live in a free democratic society where 'freedom of conscience and the free profession and practice of religion are, subject to public order and morality guaranteed to every citizen.' (Irish Constitution, Art 44.2) Religious groups have a constitutional right to exist and to propagate their brand of religion once they remain within the law.

The Southern Association of Irish Baptist Churches was particularly incensed about the harassment of minority groups by the media and others. In a statement issued in March 1983 they said: 'we are concerned about the pressure which is being exerted upon individuals and minority groups who are exercising their constitutional rights to the full profession of their religion in our pluralist society'. They went on to express their dismay at what amounts 'to a "smear campaign" which has been mounted in which brain-washing cults have been joined in the public mind with evangelical Christians.'

The Vatican Council emphasised that each person has a right to religious freedom. It stated that this freedom means 'that all men are immune from coercion on the part of individuals or of social groups and of any human power, in such wise that in matters religious no one is to be forced to act contrary to his own beliefs. Nor is anyone to be restrained from acting in accordance with his own beliefs.'[7]

Irish Catholicism must not develop an intolerance towards new evangelical groups. They attract and will continue to attract converts. All this is a challenge to the Church to develop a strategy of practical evangelisation coupled with a system of more effective pastoral care. Encouraging existing groups and associations within the Church must surely be one of the ways forward. Also of importance is the great need for an openness to the participation of the laity in the spiritual mission of the

Church. A greater emphasis on seminary training based on a recognition and fostering of the charisms of evangelisation, healing, preaching and pastoring would help to meet the new challenges posed by evangelical groups.

When a person accepts Jesus as personal Lord and Saviour there arises the need to live out this experience 'in communion' with those of like mind. There is the need for continuing support. In a very enlightened book Stephen Clark writes that 'a Christian must have an environment in his life in which Christianity is openly accepted, talked about and lived if he is going to be able to live a very vital Christian life. If he does not have this, his whole life as a Christian will be weak and might even die away. Yet fewer and fewer Catholics are finding such an environment.'[8] Evangelical groups, fellowships and 'house churches' provide such an environment. These are groups where people are willing to be more than friends. They're willing to give of themselves to support each other, and to be committed to one another. Some of the communities and fellowships I have visited contain much spiritual wisdom. The leaders of many groups have impressive pastoral skills in building community and shepherding those under their care.

The average Roman Catholic parish falls far short of the kind of Christian community we need. Even those involved in parish activities are usually only relating functionally. Those involved in spiritual ministries, for example readers or ministers of the Eucharist, are primarily in a serving capacity. Missing from the parish scene are: serious teaching to help spiritual growth; spiritual direction geared to deepen relationships with God; spiritual relationships of mutual support; regular meetings; pastoral skills in building community and shepherding. The combination of searching and seeking and a need for community which can be met by some evangelical groups are factors that can lead to a break with the Church.

Global Phenomenon

The extraordinary growth of fundamentalist evangelical groups is a world-wide phenomenon. I recall with a sense of wonder the amazing sight of the aladura gathered in their thousands on Bar Beach outside Lagos, Nigeria. Under powerful arc lamps and with sophisticated amplification they praise and worship God for hours.

In Santiago, Chile, the Pentecostals singing and praying at every street corner on a Sunday afternoon are a familiar sight.

A journalist just back from a five-week visit to Central America was struck by numerous signs of the growing presence of fundamentalist sects. She wrote: 'from purpose-built schools in the larger cities to minute shacks turned into chapels in the countryside, the signs are everywhere.' The growth of fundamentalists in Guatemala has been explosive, while in El Salvador, though no official figures are available, the author heard some estimates that sect membership may have reached 20 per cent of the population — compared with 5 per cent in 1977. A Nicaraguan refugee in southern Honduras, when asked what had caused him to abandon his Catholic faith, replied; 'the evangelical faith makes more demands on you.' What did the preacher tell them? 'Many things. They say Communism is bad — it's against the Lord.'[9]

The fundamentalist sects seem to be having the greatest success in countries which were traditionally Roman Catholic. This is evidenced by their success not just in Latin America but in European countries like Spain and France.

The greatest defence against the growth of evangelical sects is a renewed and revitalised Roman Catholic faith.

NOTES
1. Ecumenism and Charismatic Renewal, Malines Document, p. 89.
2. F.P. Moller, One in Christ *(Faith and Experience,* p. 308).
3. Leon Joseph Suenens, *A New Pentecost,* Seabury Press, p. 69.
4. Dermot A. Lane, *The Experience of God,* Veritas, 1985, p. 15.
5. Michael Paul Gallagher, *Help my Unbelief,* Veritas, 1983, p.104.
6. The *Irish Catechist,* December 1983.
7. Declaration on Religious Freedom, Ch.1, Art2.
8. Stephen B. Clark, *Building Christian Community,* Ave Maria Press, 1972,
9. *The Tablet,* 14 April 1984, p. 358.

4

PERSONAL TESTIMONY

John's Story

I decided to head west to California. That is where everything was supposed to happen. I had heard of a transcontinental bus 'The Grey Rabbit', which advertised in *The Village Voice* newspaper in New York. The total cost was $69 and the journey lasted three days and three nights. The day I was travelling about thirty people boarded the bus. The journey was rough but enjoyable. There weren't even any seats on the bus. In the course of the journey I got friendly with Maurice. His parents were Irish although he had lived all his life in London.

At 6 a.m. on a Wednesday we arrived into Market Street Station, San Francisco. We were very tired after our exhausting journey. Maurice and I decided to stick together for a few days and see what was happening around the city. I went off to the bathroom for a moment. When I returned to Maurice he said, 'you'll never guess what happened. I have met two girls who have invited me to dinner.' I said to myself — this is really San Francisco alright. 'There they are now', he said. We went over to talk to them and he introduced me. Janice was the name of one, Pam the other. Although not all that good looking, they seemed to be nice and friendly people. They were delighted to hear that we were going to view their art gallery and go for dinner with them.

If we hadn't a place to stay they could organise something, they told us. That was great because we hadn't the energy at that time in the morning to do anything. We arrived at the art gallery where we had lunch. They showed us pictures of the farm on which they were living outside San Francisco. From our conversation with them they seemed to be very happy people.

After the meal and experiencing their hospitality we couldn't very well decline to go to the farm when they suggested it. Anyway I was very curious to see what it was like. They said they were a group of young people working with the Creative Community. The main objects of the Community were to help the old in San Francisco and to assist people on drugs. They also shipped food to the Third World. The whole idea of this commune attracted me. Maurice decided to stay in San Francisco for a day or two, and I decided go with them.

We boarded a white van. There were six of us, two German girls, one New Zealand guy, two boys from the States and myself. All of us were in our early to mid-twenties. We talked a lot about travelling. I kept asking questions about the Community. Everything I was told about it seemed very nice. Later I learned that they told you what they felt you wanted to hear. They were allowed to tell 'heavenly lies' to achieve their objectives.

We arrived at the farm late at night. We stayed in the 'Chicken Palace' which was like a big hay shed. People started helping me. 'Was I OK for blankets?' they asked. I could hardly believe such nice people existed. I had no problem at all getting to sleep that night.

I woke up at 7 a.m. to the sound of one of the leaders of the community singing with guitar accompaniment. 'The red, red, robin comes bob-bob-bobbing along' he sang. We went for a morning hike. Everyone seemed to be in such fantastic humour it was incredible. People came around introducing themselves, they urged me to stay for a while. They explained how they had come for a day or two and had stayed for four, five or six months.

One or two drug addicts, one in particular I remember, Kevin was his name, told me he hadn't touched drugs for months. The mist rising from the mountains, the birds singing, the beautiful scenery, were things that really 'got' one. After the hike there was some singing and we went down to a breakfast that was laid out in the front garden on the lawn. The people beside me kept offering me some of their food. Eventually I was being offered so much that I felt I would look a terrible glutton if I took it.

Most of the leaders seemed to be aged between 25-35, very clean-shaven guys but they were not effeminate. They obviously had leadership qualities. I was impressed by the ideals presented, namely to build a new world. I was also fascinated by the fact that there was no evidence of drugs, sex or rock music.

After breakfast we were all invited to attend lectures. The initial thrust of the first lecture was that beliefs ought not to be blind. We were told 'if our understanding is based on truth we can get through strong mental blocks of thousands of years'. They dealt with questions like 'who are we'? 'Where did we come from'? 'Where are we going'? We were told that we were the missing link between creation and God.

During the day the leaders split us up into sharing groups of about ten people. The group began with introductions, followed by an open forum where one would share one's thoughts. Incidentally each new-comer was assigned a 'spiritual parent' who was to be the guide over our spiritual growth. Janice was assigned to me. She said she was very happy with me and I was a nice person. 'I was going to be a really great brother' she said. I felt that as everyone else was opening up about their innermost thoughts, why shouldn't I?

The days were taken up with lectures, discussions, playing volleyball and dodge ball, singing songs, picking fruit or other manual labour. At no stage did I detect any unhappiness in the members of 'the family' as they were called.

Many of the lectures were contradictory to the Catholic religion especially in relation to the Immaculate Conception and life after death. I was brought up to believe that 'Oh, that's a mystery of your religion'. Blind faith is satisfactory for some people, but for me, with a curious inquiring mind, it was insufficient.

In my time at the farm I met some very interesting people. I can remember one chap, a redheaded, tall, lanky youth called Myles Kavanagh. He had been a student priest. I found this an ideal opportunity to discuss religion with somebody who had obviously thought about it a lot more deeply than I had. I got into asking him questions about the Bible. These questions were always in the back of my mind but I had never had sufficient time alone with the people who really knew about it to talk to them about it.

I stayed with them for about a week. It was a very exciting week and at no stage did I really feel that I was being kept there against my will. After a week I decided, OK, this was great, everything was fantastic but I'd like to move on. Janice said 'Oh you can't move on, you can't move on, we have a weekend retreat coming up at our retreat place, Camp K. It's only $20 to go for a weekend'. I said it wasn't the money, I just wanted to push on down to Mexico and places like that. She said 'Surely you can wait another few days and go to Camp K and hear Dr Moses Durst, he is one of our best brothers and one of our best lecturers'. For the first time I had a feeling that I was being trapped, mentally imprisoned in the community. I was persuaded by two or three other members of the community that I was foolish to leave without hearing Dr Durst. I said 'OK, I'll go to Camp K for the weekend and I'll go back to San Francisco after that.'

Camp K was more heavily into religion. At the same time I was still learning so I didn't see it as that much of a disadvantage to stay. I was genuinely interested in what they were doing.

I went to Camp K. I had heard that they were members of the Unification Church, but hadn't really heard of the term 'Moonies' as such. At the Saturday night concert at the weekend retreat at Camp K, each group thought up a song suitable for a competition. Some ingenuity went into these songs and everybody racked their brains. It's amazing the fun people can have without any boozing or anything like that, just from the simple things of life, like playing volleyball. The idea was to get everybody back to their childhood days when they were in a pure state.

I stayed at Camp K for about four days and then I said 'Look, I'm pushing on. I said I was pushing on and that's it.' I wanted to get out and see more of the world. I was mentally plagued by people saying, 'Look, you have found a way of life here that means something to you', which was true, 'you've also got an explanation of the meaning of life. You have found the truth, God has called you and now you're reneging on him', they said. 'It isn't just coincidence that you left Ireland, travelled to the States and met us. That was laid out for you all along, fate had it all laid out. Why did you leave Ireland? Subconsciously or unconsciously you were looking for something and now that you have found it you are afraid to face up to the facts.' This *was* true to a certain extent. They had a very good standard of living, they were helping people.

Janice broke down when I told her I was definitely going. There was no way I was not going. Other people came around to try to persuade me to stay. Then I said I'd stay one more week, but that was it. The next day we were all at lunch and somebody asked me about registering for the week. When I went to register they said 'have you got your $50 registration fee?' Being pretty low on cash when I decided to stay for the extra week I retorted that I was never told about this. 'What, Janice never told you?' the lady said. 'No she didn't!' 'Well did Christina tell you?' 'Nobody told me'. 'That's surprising, somebody should have told you.' Obviously if they had told me the night before I wouldn't have decided to stay at all. I said 'forget it, I'm going'. I just closed my ears to the people. That gave me a way out even though I knew that it was only a very superficial way out. I was really afraid of what I was finding out.

The amount of mental pressure that was put on me to stay was really unbelievable. All the friends I had made in the last few weeks came up to me and started crying.... I really felt terrible. I said 'look I'm leaving and that's it.' I was very frustrated, very mixed up and really didn't know what to do.

Eventually they said the bus was coming that night. If I wanted I could go into town on it. As it happened the bus didn't arrive and the next bus was coming at 4 a.m. which meant that I had to stay awake all night. If I had fallen asleep I'd have missed the bus. All the way in on the bus people tried to persuade me that I was doing the wrong thing and kept hassling me.

I was really worth nothing when I got back to San Francisco. When I got back they never offered me food. I was very worried. I felt that I had experienced something that nobody had ever experienced before. I knew my place was back there with them helping people out. At least I should have stayed if I was anyway decent, for another month or two. If I had done that I would probably still be there.

My next few days in San Francisco were very uneasy. I kept on trying to meet people who would confirm that the people up in the commune were very evil people. In a sense it soothed me. I knew I was searching out people who were critical of them. I felt that these people had found a good way of life, and unknown to myself I was influenced by them. At the time I felt that they were right and the people in the outside world who were criticising them were wrong. This is what we were told in Camp K. That when we would come to town people would be criticising the creative community and the Unification Church.

Paul's Story

This girl next door was a friend of a friend of mine. I was down in my friend's house one day. The girl was there. She asked me 'do you want to come to a twig meeting? It's not religious.' 'If it's not religious', I said, 'fair enough, I'll go'. My friend brought me down on his motorbike. I went in and began talking to one of the ladies there. I was discussing the Blessed Virgin with her. We decided that the Blessed Virgin didn't need to come into religion. She began to tell me about being 'born again'. I was expecting to go on some 'big trip' when I was born again but I didn't. I just had to repeat Romans 10:9: 'If you confess with your lips that Jesus is Lord and believe in your heart that God raised him from the dead, you will be saved'. That's all there was to it.

They had this class called 'Power for Abundant Living'. They explained that 'this class teaches you how to have more abundant life'. I had no money on me. They were trying to sign me up for the course straight away. The course cost £50. I was told there was a twig in Whitehall.

I went to this meeting the very next week to see what it was like. I had been paid so I offered them £30. They refused to accept me for the class saying, 'no, you will have to wait until you have the full £50, anyway you have to sign up a week in advance of the course.' I got the £50 together but there was a delay before the next class was due to begin and then it was going to be in Ranelagh. I didn't mind because I was working in Dundrum at the time and I had just bought a motorbike on the 'never-never'.

I began the class. Many of the lectures were tape recorded talks by a Dr Paul Wierville. It was all about doubt; worry; fear; negative believing; positive believing. It went on from there to the Holy Spirit. If you ever want anything, all you have to do is believe, we were told. It didn't work. The principle sounded OK. The class taught all sorts of different principles. One of these was 'giving and receiving'. We were told to give 10 per cent of our income every week to 'The Way'. I thought that by doing this I was going to be rich, I would get it back on the double. They told us that we would get it back if not in money, in spiritual blessing. I just got more screwed up all the time.

I kept thinking that something great was going to happen in my life and so I continued to go to the meetings. I got friendly with the people there. An important part of the organisation was recruiting new people to undertake the Power for Abundant Living Course. A number of people undertook this work almost as a full-time apostolate. I decided to give up my job and join a number of other lads who were living together and witnessing in Dundalk. I moved to Dundalk and managed to get a job in a pub. I was told to leave that job so I got another job in a chipper. I didn't get on too well with the others in the house so I stayed a few months and then decided to leave. I went home. I stayed at home for a week or two. I began to feel guilty. I had failed The Way. I had let everyone down. We were always told that to leave meant that we had failed the Lord and given ourselves over to the 'evil one'. So I went back.

This time I went to Cork and moved into a house with some more members of The Way. The guy in charge arrived from Dublin. He had told me that I wasn't doing the work as I was supposed to. I didn't go out on the street and I wasn't able to get people to undertake the Power for Abundant Living Course. I was asked to leave. About this time I felt a great pressure on me. I didn't know what I was doing with my life. I felt hassled and disjointed. Everything was going wrong. I thought I would go to the university or school that The Way have in America. All the time I felt a pressure inside me. Then something snapped inside me. I just went completely off tangent. I don't know what it was. My family came and I had to go to hospital. I think I was going mad. I probably was. I was in this psychiatric hospital for months. Once I tried to set fire to the place. I felt terrible.

Now that I am out I don't feel too bad. I have no intention of going back to The Way. I stayed with them because I thought they were right. I was certain that they were going to give me something new that I had never experienced before. They didn't like the Church. All the time I was there they did nothing but point out all the faults there were in the Catholic Church. We were going back to the early Church before it had become corrupted.

I am drifting now. I have no job but I am beginning to feel a bit better inside myself. I have no intention of going back to The Way again.

5

THE CHARACTERISTICS OF CULTS

Many religious and quasi-religious groups have been classed internationally as cults. The most notorious of these are probably the Moonies, the Children of God, the Divine Light Mission and the Hare Krishna. When referring to to these groups the term 'cult' is consistently used in a derogatory fashion, invariably to denote something sinister and evil. It has been attached indiscriminately to any religious group that fails to conform to accepted norms of religious orthodoxy and practice. It has now become a 'buzz' word thrown around haphazardly by people who haven't taken sufficient time to consider their careless use of language. Much of the anger directed at some of the new religious movements is understandable. It comes from the hurt of parents and family members who have experienced the pain of separation from a loved one. The Western Bishops' Pastoral Letter 1983 expressed this as follows: 'we know that people have been upset, worried, disturbed and saddened by the separation caused even in their own families when a child or brother or sister proclaimed that they now belonged to a new religious group and rejected the Catholic Church'. Despite this I feel it is important not to issue blanket condemnations of every religious phenomenon that we do not understand or feel threatened by.

The *Oxford Dictionary* defines a cult as 'religious worship expressed in customs, ritual and ceremonies'. When I use the term in the remainder of this book it will be in the organisational sense of a particular structured group committed to certain forms of worship and behaviour. The nature of the group can then be determined by the reader from the subsequent explanation of its essential features. This is not to suggest that there aren't common areas of serious concern in relation to the methods of recruitment, the authoritarian use of power, the manipulation of largely uninformed minds, and the growing wealth and even the political involvement of many of the new religious groups.

Other people view new religious or quasi-religious groups from a different perspective. In fairness I would like to submit the definition of Daniel C. Markham, a counsellor for the Spiritual Counterfeits Project of Berkeley, California. This ministry is dedicated to educating the public on cults and aiding those who have been affected by them. He defines a cult as 'any group with an elitist cause and view of itself, who to promote their cause consciously and unconsciously abuse God-given rights and freedom of others. It is a self-seeking entity that abuses people spiritually, psychologically, physiologically, socially and theologically'.[1]

Origins

Some of the new religious groups that have appeared on the Irish scene come from the East. However, at the time of writing I cannot recall one of them that hasn't come to Ireland either directly or indirectly via America. Those with an Eastern background have been processed and packaged for Western consumption through the American religious maelstrom. One result of this is that, initially at least, funding for the new groups comes from America. The leadership in Ireland frequently retains its links with the American parent body.

There are many well-known groups of direct or indirect American origin. The Children of God was started by an evangelist, David Berg. It grew out of a coffee house ministry at Huntington Beach in California in the late 1960s. The Way International was founded by Dr Paul Wierwille, and it maintains its headquarters near Knoxville, Ohio. The Unification Church (Moonies) first appeared on the stage of the Western world on the West Coast of the United States in 1959. The Hare Krishna really began in the West when founder A.C. Bhaktivedanta Swami Prabhupada came to New York in 1977. The Divine Light Mission came to the US in 1971 when the thirteen year old Maharaji Ji set up his national and international headquarters in Denver, Colorado. They bring with them all the American entrepreneurial skills and a sizeable dose of the capitalistic philosophy that is deeply interested in money as well as souls.

In the course of preparing the material for this book I have had the opportunity of meeting participants and leaders in some of the groups already mentioned. Cult leaders are skilful at parrying most of the accusations that are levelled at them. It is possible to go away from an interview anaesthetised, almost wondering why you had come in the first place. On occasions it is difficult to be objective and to form a mature judgement. I have been given literature and tapes, have been shown films and videos. There are times when I have been overwhelmed with invitations to 'come and see' and the 'we have nothing to hide' syndrome. I have seldom encountered aggressiveness, with the exception of the 'Moonies', who dislike being challenged and generally run for cover.

The other side of the coin is the parents and friends of those who become involved with these groups. It can be such a heartbreak for families who experience the disruption of their home life by spiritual phenomena that are alien to Irish tradition and spirituality. The stories told by parents and family members contrast strongly with those told by their offspring who have joined such groups.

The parents tell of horrific personality changes, mind control, enforced asceticism, manipulation. When I presented these accusations to the leaders of the groups, to the young people in question, they have, of course, been vehemently denied.

Accusations that have been levelled at cults have also been made about groups within the Church — Opus Dei and the Legionaries of Christ for instance. The Charismatic Renewal has been accused of breaking up marriages. A 'nun running' scandal broke some years ago where it was alleged that young girls from Kerala in India were enticed to leave India and be transported to Italy to join a religious order where they would staff convents who were experiencing the 'vocation pinch'. Accusations against any religious group no matter how distorted, deserve to be examined with as much charity and honesty as possible in this difficult area.

There is a frustration on the part of parents who do not know the best attitude to adopt in the face of what appear to them to be weird 'goings-on'. It is difficult for them to obtain advice that is effective. Occasionally, kidnapping and deprogramming have been resorted to by parents or their agents. Others have tried to keep the lines of communication open and retain contact with the group and their own family member. This frequently demands a great deal of courage, sometimes even stamina.

The Self-Consciousness Movement

Since the late 1960s the Western world has gone on a binge of self-consciousness. Millions are meditating, concentrating, touching and feeling. Some claim that psychoanalysis is the answer without which one cannot be a whole person. For others it is Transcendental Meditation, psychosynthesis, bioenergetics, EST or primal therapy. Still more have been drawn into an extraordinary number of new religious groups. Each claims to belong to a special or elect group to which the divine power has paid particular attention and shows concrete signs of favour. This may be in the form of knowledge, insight into secret truth or just the saving awareness of being singled out. All make gilt-edged promises, from a good night's sleep through relaxation to a guarantee of eternal salvation. Maharishi Mahesh Yogi, the founder of Transcendental Meditation, is not to be outdone when it comes to promising goodies. He claims that 'whatever a man desires he should be able to accomplish through just twenty minutes of TM morning and evening. Life is not a struggle. It is bliss.' Some promise levitation, others astral travel. Of course nothing is free. It is an indication of the level of spiritual bankruptcy in which the Western world finds itself that the most 'way out' groups still manage to attract adherents and at a price! The Moonies' empire is reckoned to be worth $5 million. It publishes its own newspaper, *The Washington Times*. With only a handful of followers in Ireland it was able to purchase Kilworth House, a large mansion in Cork.

The Hare Krishna, with a paltry number of devotees, can maintain a large mansion in Dublin and own a large farm in Glengarrif. In Australia the Krishnas recently spent close to $1 million to run full colour promotional supplements in all the country's major newspapers. America's new architectural wonder is undoubtedly Prabhupada's Palace of Gold in West Virginia. Designed and built by Hare Krishna devotees, the palace was created as a memorial to the founder. It is gilded with 8,000 square feet of 22 carat gold leaf and included in the building are 63 tons and 40 varieties of imported marble and onyx. A leading West Virginia tourist official lists the Hare Krishna Palace of Gold as 'the top cultural attraction in the state.'[2]

Christians who believe that secular society sets the Church's priorities have encouraged some of these groups at times. I have been surprised by the facilities that have been placed at the disposal of totally counterfeit spiritual or quasi-spiritual groups by religious orders and less often by parochial clergy. On occasion I have challenged such misplaced benevolence only to be answered by a dismissive 'we thought they were alright'. Many groups cultivate local priests and sisters, sensing that Christians who take prayer seriously are likely to be generous and interested in techniques that promise to unlock spiritual power. Some groups make valiant attempts to align their public image as closely as possible with that of the main-line Christian Churches. Others, like Transcendental Meditation and the School of Philosophy and Economic Science make equally strenuous efforts to sanitise the origins and religious nature of their sect. A significant number, for instance The Way International and the Moonies, are extremely hostile to the main Christian Churches.

Some Common Features of Cults and New Religious Groups

Nearly all the cults, that is those 'religious' groups not of the mainstream major historic Churches, have certain common features. The late Monsignor Ronald Knox, surveying the development of enthusiastic sects down through the centuries of

Christianity, offered additional characteristics that were evident in historical cults. 'They are superspiritual. Their members expect more evident results from God than ordinary believers do. They are rigoristic in their demands for moral and doctrinal purity. Worldly amusements are shunned. A belief develops in the impeccability of the groups members or at least its leaders. There is an emphasis on direct personal access to God as the author of salvation. There is often an overvaluing of ecstatic religious experience.'[3]

Cult Authority

Coming from a Church that has been engaged in a process of almost continuous questioning for the past twenty years, the enforcement of authority and the demands of obedience practised in many cults is quite extraordinary. Because religious sects and cults have a compelling attraction for those seeking guidance and direction or even subordination in the form of total obedience, the 'power seekers' find ready disciples. The blind obedience demanded by the leaders and the unquestioning acquiescence given by their followers presents a new form of spiritual slavery.

The cults are extremely authoritarian in their power structure. Their leader is regarded as the supreme authority. He may delegate certain powers to a few subordinates for the purpose of seeing that the members adhere to the leader's wishes or rules. There is no appeal outside the group to a wider system of justice. Cults, through a system of pastoral counselling, frequently demand a total revelation of conscience to the leader or his subordinates. Marriages may be arranged for disciples by the leaders, as often happens in the Hare Krishna and the Moonies.

Authority is enforced by peer group pressure, fear, or even by a system of spying. One well-known cult in Ireland tours the summer pop festival circuit. They do this to sell literature and to recruit new members. An irate father described to me how his son had been 'imprisoned' in the group's van for three hours for a minor infringement of the rules laid down by the leaders. It was only intervention by the parents that secured his 'release'.

Christ's farewell discourse to his disciples illustrates the free nature of the relationship that ought to exist between master and disciple: 'No longer do I call you servants, I have called you friends' *(Jn 15:15)*. To the new Christians of Galatia Paul wrote: 'so through God you are no longer a slave but a son and if a son then an heir'. He also told them that 'Christ set us free to live in freedom, stand firm then and do not let the yoke of slavery be imposed on you again' *(Gal 5:1)*.

Cult Leaders

Cults make claims of divinity for their human leaders. They say 'Jesus was the incarnation of the divinity for his day, our leader is the reincarnation of the divinity for our time'. So the Divine Light Mission claims divinity for Guru Maharaji and the Unification Church make similar claims of divinity on behalf of Sun Myung Moon. Perhaps it would be more accurate to phrase it in the negative: 'they don't deny the possibility of divinity to their human leaders'. Some years ago I met the leader of a large Yoga organisation together with two of his associates. I clearly remember that the two young men who accompanied him suggested that he might be the reincarnation of Jesus Christ.

Cult leaders keep the forms of love, devotion and allegiance to themselves. It is difficult to appreciate the magnetism of a Jim Jones who, with apparent ease, persuaded over 900 people to commit voluntary suicide. In 1969, at the direction of self-proclaimed messiah, Charles Manson, three young women brutally murdered actress Sharon Tate and four guests. How did Charles Manson turn former high school cheerleaders into obedient mass murderers? Sun Myung Moon has consistently managed to preside over arranged mass marriages, some involving up to eight hundred couples, in Madison Square Garden in New York.

The Pennsylvania Conference on Inter-Church cooperation, a body made up of the Pennsylvania Council of Churches and the Pennsylvania Catholic Conference, in a statement on 'the dangers of pseudo-religious cults', noted that 'each cult has a messianic type leader who claims to have received a new, ultimate and final revelation from God'.[4]

My experience is that it is difficult even to speak to individual cult members without the local leader being present to monitor the conversation. Even in the presence of the leaders most of the conversation is mediated through him by a series of interjections and explanations.

The presence of the leader is pervasive. He is leader and teacher, supervisor and spiritual master. He is the one who unlocks the knowledge so eagerly sought by the disciple. Almost all cults and pseudo-religious groups focus on a cult figure or guru rather than on God.

Love Bombing

The term 'love bombing' has been used to describe the recruitment strategy adopted by many cults. It is a process of uncritical acceptance and exaggerated kindness designed to lure potential recruits into a rapid relationship of dependence on the group or one of its members. Psychological techniques combined with superspiritual language encourage the potential recruit to suspend, at least temporarily, his critical faculties. New recruits experience being totally loved and accepted. 'Everybody is nice, it's unbelievable' they think. A typical example of 'love bombing' is contained in John's testimony in an earlier chapter of this book.

I think the power of love bombing has been exaggerated. It is little more than a Dale Carnegie 'How to Win Friends and Influence People' process used for a spurious spiritual purpose.

What is the difference between 'love bombing' and a vocation workshop run by the Catholic Church in Ireland? Experience has shown that a vocation that is not a free response to God and to a life of service will compound existing problems for the candidate and for the religious order and diocese.

At a vocation workshop the elements of sacrifice and self-denial in the lives of priests and religious are emphasised. A potential candidate who entertained any doubts about the validity of a vocation would be encouraged to wait for a period and test his vocation. Love bombing removes all obstacles immediately and presents the cult as an answer to all one's problems. A trouble free life is the nirvana promised.

Doctrine

There is little similarity between the doctrines of the cults. They range from pseudo-Christian through meditation techniques to forms of Hinduism. There is, however, a common perspective through which each cult views its own doctrine.

The attempt to reduce all belief and behaviour to a single narrow pattern is another symptom of the religious power seekers at work. The doctrinal absolutism of cults identifies acceptability, if not salvation itself, with unconditional adherence to complex ideals of belief and morality elaborated by self-appointed legislators. It boils down to the assertion that only one way is the true way — our way. This usually has the hidden insistence that dissent, divergence or alternatives are not only out of the question but downright evil and dangerous.

Their claim is to provide simple, indeed simplistic solutions to the most complex problems of life. They have an answer for every question. They see themselves as a fellowship of the saved rather than a mixture of saints and sinners. Sinners are excommunicated and even shunned. Not for these groups the doubts against faith of a St Thérèse or any echo of the prophet Isaiah — 'truly you are a hidden God'.

Asceticism

Many cults and new religious movements encourage a rigorous asceticism for new members. This asceticism is particularly attractive to young people as it is the antithesis of the lax commitment to their faith demonstrated by some of their parents. Vegetarian meals and particular brands of 'health foods' rapidly become their staple diet to the confusion and consternation of parents. Douglas Hyde, an ex-communist and former editor of *The Daily Worker*, commented on similar tactics used on new recruits to communism. In his book *Dedication and*

Leadership he writes: 'Communists have proved, as others have done too, that to commit people publicly, to make them at the time of their first early enthuasism do something which involves some degree of moral courage, which brings them before others in their new role, and submits them to the possibility of attack, can be of profound significance.'[5]

It has been alleged of one of the new sects that it deprives members of nourishing food in order to create a dependence on the movement. It is a fact that their diet is very restricted, with the only source of protein being nuts, grains and vegetables. Also, they rise at 4 a.m. for meditation and prayer. I am convinced that the use of severe penitential exercise does help the leaders of some groups to gain further control over their devotees. Plunging new recruits into severe and prolonged penance certainly increases the possibility of their manipulation. On occasions the Moonies have used a combination of severe fasting and exhausting night vigils as a means of breaking down resistance in potential converts.

Brainwashing

Accusations of brainwashing have consistently been levelled at the cults. I think it must be admitted that over the centuries leaders of successive religions have used a combination of fear, fasting, physical discipline, breathing exercises, incense, music and drumming for religious purposes. I recall my first experience of the Spiritual Exercises of St Ignatius and the meditations on hell. Somerset Maugham describes this in more graphic detail than I could — 'with the eyes of his fancy the penitent must see the terrible flames and the souls enclosed as it were in bodies of fire. "Look", Fr Raymond cries "Look at the unhappy creatures writhing in the burning flames, their hair standing on end, their eyes staring out of their heads, their aspect horrible, biting their hands ... if in your soft bed it is so painful to you to pass a long night of sleeplessness and pain, waiting eagerly for relief of dawn, what will you feel in that eternal night upon which the dawn never breaks, during which you will never have an instant of refreshment, during which you will never see a ray of hope".'[6]

It is not so long ago in Ireland that fear certainly produced conformity. Was this brainwashing?

John Wesley, the spiritual father of more than thirty-five denominations, the largest being the United Methodist Church, 'would create high emotional tension in his potential converts. He found it easy to convince large audiences of that period that a failure to achieve salvation would necessarily condemn them to hell fire for ever and ever.'[7]

Many of the *aladura* (Pentecostal-type) churches and fellowships of Africa use a concentration of heavy drumming and a whipped-up and heightened sense of expectation to produce 'religious' effects.

Many religions have made a practise of inducing guilt and acute apprehension as the first step towards conversion. Some insisted that 'the tension must be increased until the sinner broke down and made complete submission to the will of God.'[8]

I understand brainwashing to mean the use of proselytising techniques that aim at the systematic erosion and reversal of a person's habits or convictions against their will and by the use of prolonged stress. The goal is attitude change, and the subject has to be put into a psychological state of suggestibility. One commentator, speaking in another context, claims that 'to achieve this end the captors may use drugs, food and sleep deprivation, repeated terrorising, interrogations and ideological arguments.'[9] The same authors highlight the fact that with the most sophisticated techniques the Chinese communists failed lamentably in their efforts to 'brainwash' US service men in the Korean War. Of the 3,500 American POWs captured during the Korean War only about fifty made pro-communist statements and only twenty-five refused to be repatriated when the war ended. A pathetic 1 per cent was the fruit of their efforts!

I do not believe that the cults use systematic coercive or psychological techniques deliberately and against the will of a potential recruit any more than do groups within the Church. Accusations have been made against Opus Dei of virtual house arrest. One testimony against that organisation claimed 'I was constantly supervised, allowed no mail or telephone calls and I was regularly interrogated by priests.'[10] Another writer alleged that 'it took many hours of soul-searching on my part before I realised I had been seriously misled into joining a sect with 'Moonies-type' brainwashing .... I was told by the Opus Dei hierarchy when I acquainted them of my intention of leaving that I would be damned, never to get to Heaven.

My experience is that all of these charges of brainwashing are grossly exaggerated. I am acquainted with ex-cult members who had little difficulty leaving the group *when they wanted to.*

The accusations of brainwashing often arise when there is a conflict between parents and the group members. Parents find it difficult to understand why their wishes are not being obeyed. They deeply resent the hold the group seems to have over their youngster. They themselves find the ideology and behaviour of the group so distasteful that it seems absolutely inexplicable that their child could be there voluntarily. There is also the added burden of guilt. Parents ask themselves where they have failed. Fear, anger and frustration understandably lead them to make accusations that make the situation more tolerable to bear. One parent whose daughter has belonged to one of the most notorious cults for a number of years said that she did not believe that her daughter was brainwashed but that her joining the group was a 'cop-out'.

There is a large turnover of membership in most of the cults. This in itself seems to belie the accusation of brainwashing. I am acquainted with a number of ex-cult members who are now re-established in 'straight society'. They left because of boredom or dislike of the tasks that they were asked to perform or because of the authoritarian style of the leadership or simply because they had managed to meet a companion outside the group with whom they wished to have an ongoing relationship.

I know that the cults will make every effort to retain their members. There will be psychological pressure to stay. They will be dubbed failures if they leave. One member of The Way International told me that he left twice before he was finally able to break his links with the cult. He said 'it was O.K. for the first week after I left. Then I began to have doubts about my motives for leaving. I felt a failure. I was aware of the stigma within the group that attached to anyone who left. On the two occasions I returned to the group it was because I didn't want to be a failure! I would say there is pressure, perhaps heavy pressure, but "brainwashing" — no'.

Community

Undoubtedly the trump card played by all the new religious groups is the building of a community of love where all will live in relationships of brotherhood. In the early days of the Children of God it was impressive to experience the level of commitment within the group. At the time they had very little to live on but the little they had they shared. There was a very high level of identification with the group. Singing, praying, sharing and living together contributed to an exciting family life.

The same was true of the Divine Light Mission. The good of the individual was always subject to the good of the group as a whole. A group of young people living together, sharing a common cause, protecting itself from the onslaughts of a hostile 'world', believing itself to be specially selected or highly favoured by God, all produced a solidarity that was exciting and appealing to young people. Home life was very stuffy in comparison. It was interesting to observe youngsters undertaking the most menial of chores, chores that they would be unlikely to perform in their own homes. The order that was needed to live in reasonable harmony was not generally resented. Even today, the Hare Krishna will give glowing testimonies of their blissful community life together.

It is not easy to detach young people from this type of community life style. When they first begin to flirt with a religious group they are generally encouraged to drop their present commitments and relationships. Over a period of time they drop one set of relationships and patterns of behaviour and form new ones. Of course this means that without knowing it they are becoming more and more dependent on the group for the very sustenance of healthy living. Even if they wanted to leave the prospect is daunting. Who do they go to? Leaving home in the first place could have been an escape from pressure or from a difficult family situation. It is sometimes easier for them to stay than to leave.

'The world is the enemy' new recruits will have been told. 'You have found the truth. God has specially selected you. The poor people in the world are in error. They are not saved like us. Obviously when God is doing such a marvellous thing in our group Satan will come and try to rob you of this gift. He will use any wiles. He will even use your parents. He will use your former friends.'

Elitism

The belief that only a small number of specially privileged souls are truly capable of enlightenment and ultimately of salvation is the form of elitism firmly practised by most cults. With elitism goes a persuasive spiritual arrogance which despairs of the great mass of people who have not yet received enlightenment and who probably never will. Roy Wallis, in a most enlightening book, emphasises this point: 'they construe themselves as alone possessed of a truth relevant to every aspect of human existence, embracing the individual totally and the whole of society. Since there exists certainty as to their truth, there can be no compromising or temporising with other ideas. Members are expected to turn completely from alternative sources of belief, to embrace the truth unreservedly and to recognise that truth lies solely within the community of believers. It must therefore be defended against error and converts must display a high level of commitment and loyalty before complete acceptance, and work assiduously to spread such an important message to the world or assist in its being brought to fruition.'[12]

The form of elitism includes a criticism of established historical religions and a general willingness to enter into debate. They *know* why everything in the Church is wrong.

Characteristics of Groups that represent a threat to Young People

(a) Restrict contact with relatives or friends.
(b) Forbid or discourage the use of spiritual direction from a source outside the group.

(c) Forbid any exercise of dissent or divergence particularly where such dissent is forbidden under the pain of expulsion.

(d) Make promises to endow disciples with special powers of healing, levitation, psychic abilities or physical skills beyond the ordinary.

(f) Use electronic instruments or psychological manipulation to produce altered states of consciousness which would be indentified in advance with divine visitations.

(g) Distinguish between the moral behaviour of the leaders and that of disciples especially in matters of sexuality and also in regard to luxurious lifestyle.

(h) Alignment, directly or indirectly, with a political party of government.

(i) Predict the imminent end of the world.

(j) Unreasonable or pathological hostility to existing main-line Christian Churches.

NOTES

1. Daniel C. Markham, *Cults and Cultism* (Unpublished manuscript).
2. *Who Are They*, Bhaktivedanta Book Trust, 1982.
3. Ronald Knox, *Enthusiasm*, Clarendon Press, 1950.
4. *Doctrine and Life,* December 1981.
5. Douglas Hyde, *Dedication and Leadership,* Notre Dame Press, 1966, p. 71.
6. William Somerset Maugham, *Don Fernando*, Heinemann, 1950, 1957.
7. William Sargant, *Battle for the Mind,* Pan 1957, p. 84.
8. *Battle for the Mind*, p. 132.
9. Bromly and Shupe, *Strange Gods – The Great American Cult Score*, Beacon Press, 1981, p. 99.
10. Dr John J. Roche, Linacre College, Oxford.
11. *Der Spiegel*, 5 September 1983.
12. Roy Wallis, *The Elementary Forms of the New Religious Life*, Routledge and Kegan Paul, 1984, p. 126.

6

A CATALOGUE OF CULTS

Unification Church (Moonies)

It is difficult to give an accurate summary of the doctrines of the Unification Church. It is a hotchpotch of Christianity, Taoist philosophy, spiritism and anti-communism blended to produce Rev. Sun Myung Moon as the Messiah for his age. The basic work containing the supposed revelations given to Moon is entitled *The Divine Principle*.

The Unification Church was founded in Korea in 1954. It claims to have over 3 million followers in 120 countries. Moon was born into a Presbyterian family in the Pyungan Buk-do province of what is now North Korea. He claims to have received divine revelation in 1936 indicating that he was destined to accomplish a great mission in which Jesus would work with him. After achieving success with his new religion in the Far East, Moon came to America in 1971.

Doctrine

The doctrines of the Unification Church appear utterly bizarre and seem to defy real understanding. They teach that Eve sinned not by eating of the fruit, but by being sexually seduced by Satan, who until then was an unfallen angel. This seduction resulted in the fall of Satan and of mankind. On realising that God wanted Adam to be her husband she had sexual relations with Adam, but because he was spiritually immature, this led to the physical fall of mankind.

Moon teaches that everything in creation is in a male-female, positive-negative relationship. His initial plan for man was that the perfected Adam should marry Eve and by her, fill the earth with perfect children, hence bringing into being the Kingdom of God on earth. However Satan's successful seduction of Eve effectively put paid to that plan and as a result, a specific period of time had to elapse before God's plan of redemption could come about.

God had meant Jesus Christ to live on, marry the perfect 'Eve' and produce a race of perfect children. After the dreadful mistake of Christ's death, God had to choose another race to work out his plan. They were to be prepared for the next Adam who would come and put everything right again. Moon teaches that this second Adam, known as the Lord of the Second Advent, was foretold by Christ. It is generally accepted in Moonie circles that Moon himself is the promised Lord. The doctrines are contained in *The Divine Principle*, the 'bible' of the Unification Church.

The crucial difference between Moonies and Christians is in their attitude to the person, life and death of Jesus. Moon declares things about Jesus for which there is no biblical basis.

What are Moon's aims? Briefly, he intends to amalgamate all the Christian denominations with the other great world religions such as Hinduism and Islam to form a world Church.

In October 1981 Moon was indicted by a federal grand jury in New York on charges of filing false income tax returns. The indictment alleged he had not reported $60,000 in interest earned on bank account deposits from 1973-78. In 1984 he began serving an eighteen-month sentence for income tax evasion at Dansbury Prison, Connecticut.

Evaluation

Many books have been written on the Unification Church. The vast majority are polemical in tone and intention. In this brief evaluation I will rely heavily on the research of Eileen Barker of the Department of Sociology of the London School of Economics. For three years she carried out a study on the Unification Church with the help of a grant from the Social Science Research Council of Great Britain. Her research was carried out through in-depth interviews, observation through living in Moonie centres and attending workshops and through an evaluation of a 41-page questionnaire given to all British members of the movement.

She estimated that there were 600 British members working full-time for the movement in 1980. She adds that 'there has been a growing number of "Home Church" members. These are people who accept the truth of the Divine Principle but remain associate members living at home rather than devoting their whole life to the movement.'

She mentions that members usually donate most if not all their worldly possessions to the Church. They also raise funds by selling plants or paintings or literature. Like the Hare Krishna, my experience is that this fundraising is done blatantly under false pretences. They collect 'for the starving in India' or for 'world peace'. In actual fact the funds collected go directly into the coffers of the group. The Moonies, like the Divine Light Mission, sell ginseng tea and health foods. Again there is unlikely to be any way of knowing who is behind these commercial enterprises. Shops have been opened in Dublin, the profits of which go to fund the activities of pseudo-religious groups.

The usually staid London *Times* asked with some justification 'is the Unification Church a fudge religion or a business network?' According to the article by Diana Patt, Sun Myung Moon controls an international business empire of about £6 million a year.

Deception is not confined to fundraising. In 1981 the Moonies were deeply involved in a seven-day fast for peace and in obtaining signatures in Dublin, Belfast and five other cities and towns for a declaration opposing violence as a means of solving the Northern Ireland problem. It was suspected with some justification that this was being used as a ruse to recruit new members. At that time they used posters and leaflets indicating that the campaign was organised by 'The Association for a Moral and Ethical Society'.

Brainwashed Youth?

Controversy has followed the Unification Church like a shadow. It has been unable to shake off allegations of brainwashing, mind control and indoctrination. Undoubtedly new recruits to the Moonies are expected to attend long hours of lectures, prayer and discussion. Isolated from the outside world they receive an intense and systematic grounding in the Divine Principle.

Adversaries allege that young adult recruits are subjected to a rigorous regime of deprivation of sleep, excessive fasting, constant discussion. They claim that they have been brainwashed. The Church contends they have been converted.

My experience was with a clergyman who joined the Moonies. His personal life was always disciplined, he was an intense and angry man. I was dumbfounded that a person who had been subjected to a long philosophical and theological training could 'snap' within the course of days and accept a new theology inimical to accepted Christianity. Was he brainwashed? I have no doubt that something was triggered off inside him that anaesthetised his former life and belief. To the best of my knowledge he is still an influential member of the Unification Church in America almost ten years later.

The term 'brainwashed' implies force and captivity. A person freely attending a lecture may be persuaded, lulled, conned or bamboozled, but providing he has freely come and may freely leave, he cannot be brainwashed. Eileen Barker asserts that 'it is just not true that most or even a significant number join the new religious movements under conditions of physical coercion. Only rarely can drugs be held responsible for the actual conversion. Nor can it reasonably be said that sensory deprivation through lack of sleep or poor food would provide an adequate explanation.' She suggests that certain factors must be considered when determining what leads someone to decide to join the Moonies. There are: (1) the predispositions of the person; (2) his presuppositions about his life in society; (3) the alternatives offered by the movement and; (4) the social context within which the decision whether or not to join is made.[1]

In April 1981, after a six-month jury trial, the Moonies lost an important case to the *Daily Mail*. The jury unanimously decided that the *Daily Mail* had been justified in accusing the Moonies of brainwashing converts and breaking up families. Despite this decision the Charity Commissioners decided that the organisation could continue as a registered charity. The Commission said that 'the objects of the Holy Spirit Association of World Christianity and the Sun Myung Moon Foundation were exclusively charitable in law.'

Accusations and counter-allegations have always accompanied the Moonies. My opinion is that there is some justification for charges of deception in recruitment, love bombing and rigorous discipline. I believe that accusations of brainwashing are, if true at all, grossly exaggerated.

The average British Moonie is in his late twenties, having joined at twenty-three years of age. Two thirds of the membership is male and the members come from the middle class. Most of the members have reached a high level of education, with two thirds having reached at least A levels. Eileen Barker's research showed that 'one fifth of the members were brought up as Catholics, a quarter as non-Conformists, 40 per cent as Anglicans and 4 per cent as agnostics or atheists. New recruits shared a disillusionment with the established Churches 'many of them complaining of the hypocrisy they see in the pulpit and in the congregation.'[2]

In relation to the Moonies' Irish operation it is difficult to acquire accurate information. They have moved their headquarters on several occasions and Mr Bob Duffy, who headed the Irish operation, has now left the country.

The Way International

The Way International or Power for Abundant Living is headed by Victor Paul Wierwille, a former Evangelical and reformed minister of doubtful credentials. Wierwille was born on 31 December 1916. Like Moon he claims God spoke to him on 5 October 1942. God told him he would teach him the true New Testament doctrines. Wierwille tells us: 'I was praying ... and that's when He said He would teach me the Word as it has not been known since the first century, if I would teach it to others.'[3]

Wierwille, who is revered within The Way International as a scripture scholar of international repute, hardly measures up to this judgement. He received his BA degree from Mission House College, Plymouth in 1938 and a ThB from the same school in

1940. In 1948 he received a PhD degree from Pike's Peak Bible Seminary, an institution not known internationally for the quality of its teaching.

Doctrine

It is not clear, at first glance, that The Way International is 'a spiritual counterfeit'. The members of The Way International profess a belief in God, the Bible, Jesus Christ, salvation. The Way International express their doctrines in the same terminology as orthodox Christians. However it is clear from careful study that they do not mean the same things by the words. It is also clear that they do not share a common faith with mainstream Christian Churches. It is easy to understand that young adults not totally conversant with their own faith could be deceived by the spurious teachings of The Way International.

Wierwille claims to have done years of independent biblical research and to have rediscovered what the original Apostles taught, a teaching 'lost' to Christianity until its recovery by him.

Wierwille's basic concept is that God is one in substance and only one in person. For him the concept of the Trinity is a misinterpretation of the Greek usage in Scripture. The one person is the Father. The Holy Spirit is the Father (God) by another name, just as 'Dick' and 'Richard' can be two names for the same person. Jesus Christ is not God. Jesus Christ is called the 'son of God' because the Father fathered him in Mary's womb. Again, according to The Way International, Christ was crucified on a Wednesday, in order to make sure that he rested three full days in the grave.

In my opinion, in his interpretation of the Bible, Wierville alters scripture, ignores context, inserts his own rules, makes arbitrary judgements and statements in order to support his authority and prove his pre-conceived theology. He has gone to considerable lengths to destroy biblical evidence and no reputable Bible scholar would give a shred of credence to Wierwille's teaching.

In many respects I believe The Way International is the most insidious of all the new pseudo-religious groups. Its teaching seems to align itself so closely to main-line Christianity that it is tailored to deceive. I have had a number of meetings with members of The Way International. It is a real sadness to experience young people accepting as true the most bizarre and corrupted interpretation of scripture. The young people I have met have been unshakeable in their conviction that they had received the truth. The Way International is unlike the Moonies in that it attracts those of a low intellectual calibre and it has few effective apologists. Its members seem to memorise particular phrases of scripture and couple the text with a spurious explanation quoting Greek and Hebrew sources. Within the general hotchpotch of error, many of the central doctrines of Christianity are adhered to, such as the Virgin Birth, the Resurrection, and the Atonement.

There is a particular emphasis on 'speaking in tongues' within the organisation. This phenomenon must be accompanied by 'interpretation'. This is done to order within a prayer meeting. For instance the leader may say 'Paul, will you speak in a tongue?' Paul will promptly oblige. 'Rita, will you interpret?' Rita interprets with some message of love or encouragement as coming from God.

The Way International is adept at collecting money from its members. This is done through a system of tithing. Members are expected to give 10 per cent of their income. The courses on 'Power for Abundant Living' are expensive, taking into consideration the quality of the teaching and the 'scholarship' of the teachers.

The Way is very antagonistic to traditional Christianity. The members are subjected to constant criticism of the Church. In no time a hostility builds up towards the Churches. This hostility is not underpinned by a serious critical analysis of the Church.

Structure

The Way International is structured to resemble a tree. The 'root' or headquarters is located at a farm in New Knoxville, Ohio, where Dr Wierwille lives. 'Trunks' are countries or states. 'Branches' are areas of organisation under branch leaders. An individual meeting is a 'twig'; the members are 'leaves'.

The Way International, also known as Word over the World, has been successful in recruiting an increasing number of young Irish boys and girls. An organisation like this underlines how important it is for parents to check out the type of Bible class their son or daughter may be attending.

The Hare Krishna Movement

Some years ago a member of the Hare Krishna sect was charged with obstructing Grafton Street. On that occasion the Justice made some personal remarks about the robes of the defendant. Since then the Hare Krishna have seldom been out of the news. Recently the Revenue Commissioners took away the group's charitable status leaving them with considerable tax problems. The climax in a series of disasters was a judgment delivered in the High Court in Dublin which held that the Hare Krishna was in breach of contract in failing to complete the purchase of a large hotel in Co. Longford. The hotel was to have been used by the group as a retreat centre.

Doctrine

The Hare Krishna movement has roots in India. The scriptural source for this monotheistic tradition is the Sanskrit Vedic literature, among which are the oldest religious writings known to man. The most important of these is the *Bhagavad-gita*.

The founder of the modern Hare Krishna movement also known as the International Society for Krishna Consciousness (ISKCON) was Prabhupada, a prosperous pharmacist from Calcutta. In 1944 Prabhupada attempted to express his religious ideas in English in a magazine called *Back to the Godhead*. His work with this periodical was successful. At the age of fifty-eight he renounced his wife and five children, abandoned his business and donned the saffron robes of a Hindu monk.

In 1965 he went to America where he founded ISKCON in 1968. The Hare Krishnas grew rapidly into a worldwide confederation of spiritual centres, temples, rural communities, schools and institutions. Prabhupada has successfully packaged a Hindu philosophy for Western consumption.

Swami Prabhupada receives the honour due to God, because it was claimed by devotees that he was God's 'via media' (representative) distributing the unalloyed love of God. He said of himself that because he was carrying out God's orders, he should receive as much respect as God.[4]

Salvation for Krishna devotees is having a personal relationship with Krishna. Krishna means God. The process of chanting the Hare Krishna mantra — 'Hare Krishna, Hare Krishna, Krishna, Krishna Krishna, Hare Hare/Hare Rama, Rama Rama, Hare Hare, — revives Krishna consciousness. Krishna is awakened by chanting. Hare means 'O energy of the Lord' and Krishna means 'O Lord Krishna'.

Chanting is one of the most important rituals of the ISKCON liturgy. It is also the aspect of the Hare Krishna movement which is best known to the outside world. The chanting of this ancient formula is of course an invocation of specific Hindu deities. It is also a kind of psychological conditioning. Another significant feature of the Hare Krishna practice is their regular temple ceremonies. The most important of these relate to worshipping and attending to the 'needs' of several deity statues. These idols are presented with food, incense, a fan, a handkerchief and an offering of flowers.

The Hare Krishna leaders exercise strict discipline over their followers even to the extent of arranged marriages. The cult also tends to extinguish a person's individuality. Salvation is attained through purification by complete surrender in devotion to Krishna. As Christ is to Christians, Krishna is to Krishna devotees. He is their personal saviour.

Accusations of brainwashing have constantly been levelled against the Hare Krishna. I do not accept these accusations. We live in a society in which every effort is made to control or change other people's ideas. If people insist on using the term 'brainwashing' then they have the responsibility of defining what exactly this means. It is such a loaded term that it shouldn't be used indiscriminately. Even advertising could be cited as an example of brainwashing.

Because of the general 'high profile' of the Hare Krishna it is difficult but not impossible to trick or deceive people into joining.

The saffron robes and shaved heads of the men and the saris of the women make them easily recognisable. So what makes people join? Late in 1983 I carried out a series of interviews with Hare Krishna devotees. The testimonies highlighted the fact that they were all seeking. Few knew what they were looking for, but the Hare Krishna seemed to answer, at least for a time, a felt need. However I know that of some parents believe that their son or daughter was looking for a 'cop out'. Joining the Hare Krishna was an exciting escape from pressure of exams, school or even domestic difficulties.

The Hare Krishna are very strict vegetarians. They do not eat meat, fish or eggs. They do not smoke, nor do they drink alcohol, tea or coffee. Extra-marital sex is forbidden and even within marriage, sex is confined to fertile periods and thus only for the purpose of conception.

The ISKCON owns or controls over a hundred spiritual centres, temples and rural communities. From where does the money come to fund this enterprise? It is fairly common knowledge that the Hare Krishna don wigs, put on civilian clothing and beg on the streets of all the major cities of the world. They beg under false pretences and this has been confirmed to me. A collection for Bangladesh or the starving poor of India will most likely be used to support the activities of the local temple. In addition they sell literature and candles, and run vegetarian restaurants.

It is the element of deception that most disturbs me in all of these new pseudo-religious groups. The theory is impressive but the practice is often worldly, one might even say dishonest.

Transcendental Meditation

It's happening all over the country, and people are jumping at the chance to get into something which 'can be learnt easily and can be enjoyed by everyone' and which allegedly 'provides deep rest as a basis for dynamic action'; 'improves clarity of perception'; 'develops creative intelligence'; 'expands awareness' and 'ensures full development of the individual in a natural way'. What more could anyone want?

The 'capital of the world' has been established in the former Grand Hotel at Seelisberg, a Swiss mountain resort overlooking Lake Lucerne. This is the centre of the Transcendental Meditation Movement. TM claims to have 300 million adherents in 140 countries.

The originator of TM was Lord Krishna who gave this meditation technique to the warrior Arjuna some 5,000 years ago. Within 2,000 years its practice had fallen into disuse. In our generation Brahmanand Saraswati Maharaj (better known as Shri Guru Dev) revived this teaching. He passed it on to his favourite pupil, the Maharishi Mahesh Yogi.

The testimonies of two participants in TM may help to clarify the meditation technique.

Bernadette: In May 1976 I paid £25.00 for a TM course at the Ailesbury Road Centre. There were a couple of introductory talks at which we were assured that TM was a purely scientific technique, with absolutely no religious undertones. I went along to my initiation ceremony with the necessary white hankie and two white flowers, feeling utterly ridiculous.

My initiator took me into a room reeking of incense. I was then asked to remove my shoes. I put my hankie, some fruit and flowers on an altar in front of a picture of a Guru. There were candles on the altar, all very religious looking. My initiator knelt, closed her eyes, put her hands in a prayerful attitude and started to chant. A few minutes later she turned to me and said 'harim'. This was to be my special mantra, a 'meaningless' sound, the constant repetition of which would lead me into a 'state of greater and greater charm'.

My initiator then stood up, took my hands and intertwined them with the flowers and hankie, held my hands in hers, and chanted again for a few minutes. Then I was put into another room to meditate for a while.

There was another group session a few days later. We were finished with the TM centre, although we could ring at any time and make an appointment if we were having trouble with our technique. My mind wandered a lot, so I went back often for 'checking'. Twice during this time tapes were played to a group of us in which the Maharishi told us he could solve all our problems. This disturbed me, as did the obvious adoration all the instructors had for this Maharishi. I stopped going to the centre.

Tony: I went along to the TM centre, paid £35.00 and was enrolled as a student under a teacher named Peter. I thought that TM might help me to pray.

I had an introductory talk and was asked to return with an offering of a white handkerchief, some fruit and flowers. On my next visit Peter asked me to remove my shoes, as he had already done. He led me into a room, and while I sat in an arm-chair, he burned some incense before a picture of Maharishi Mahesh Yogi, popularly called the Maharishi. Peter intoned a long chant and then told me my mantra, a word of two syllables which meant nothing to me, but sounded like 'ken-ing'. He asked me to repeat it several times, which I did. We then practised a meditation together.

All this lasted about fifteen minutes and that was it. I was given back my hankie and fruit and went home. My fee entitled me to come back for three further practice meditations and a question and answer session with a large group.

On my return to the centre each week I was asked to fill in a form which had questions about the length of time I meditated, whether other people had noticed an improvement in my behaviour. I had to answer no to the latter. This questionnaire turned me off a bit, since it seemed a subtle way of suggesting to me that these good things should really be happening to me, because they were happening to others.

If I persisted long enough at it I could even learn to 'fly'. On the walls of the TM centre I saw pictures of people flying, that is sitting cross legged in mid-air, totally unsupported. To learn that I would have to undertake a course in Switzerland.

I carried on with my daily meditation and while it did me no harm it certainly did not change my life in any way. I began to think how foolish it was to be sitting there doing nothing when I could be praying.

I suppose I could say in favour of my little excursion into TM that it gave me a discipline in setting aside a time each day for prayer.

Doctrine:

TM is first and foremost a meditation technique. Every meditator is given a 'mantra'. He closes his eyes. After about thirty seconds the mantra should come into the mind on its own. If it doesn't happen then the meditator begins to repeat it gently to himself. There are no rules except the concentrated use of the mantra, which incidentally, is never to be divulged to anyone. Meditation cannot be forced. 'If you list instructions, you can't do it', said one instructor. 'It is like falling asleep. You can tell someone what he has to do but that is all.'

According to a *Time* magazine cover story on TM in 1975, 25 per cent of people who try TM give it up after a while. It is claimed that TM is beneficial in so far as it results in a fall in blood pressure; lower consumption of oxygen; less dependency on cigarettes, alcohol and drugs.

Why TM and Christianity do not Mix

The Transcendental Meditation programme as promoted by Maharishi Mahesh Yogi claims to be a purely secular, scientific and non-religious technique. However, on 12 December 1977, the United States District Court of New Jersey ruled that TM and the 'puja' ceremony are all religious in nature within the context of the Establishment Clause of the First Amendment and 'the teaching thereof in New Jersey public schools is therefore unconstitutional'. In commenting on the 'puja' the presiding judge said that Guru Dev 'is portrayed as a personification of a divine being or essence'. One former TM instructor, Gregory J. Randolph, said in an affidavit submitted to the court, 'we were taught to give the definite and deliberate impression to the general public and to individuals we initiated that there are a very large number of mantras and that each meditator receives a mantra which is individually chosen for him and is uniquely suited to his personality. In actual fact, each teacher has a list of sixteen mantras which are then assigned to meditators on the basis of age classification'. Other meditators have determined that the mantra is always the Sanskrit name of a Hindu God.

Maharishi has stated repeatedly that 'it's not a religion' but he has written bluntly elsewhere that 'TM is a path to God' and 'is a very good form of prayer'.

The initiation ceremony includes a prayer chanted in Sanskrit which is translated as follows:

'To the personified glory of the Lord, to Shankara, emancipator of the world I bow down. To Shankaracharya, the redeemer, hailed as Krishna and Badanayana, to the commentator of the Brahma Sutras, I bow down ... white as camphor, kindness incarnate, the essence of creation garlanded with Brahman, ever dwelling in the lotus of my heart, the creative impulse of cosmic life, to that, in the form of Guru Dev, I bow down'.

If TM is a purely secular relaxation discipline, why is there such insistence on the initiation ceremony. And isn't there something odd, even sadly amusing, about a Christian man or woman sitting in meditation repeating the name of some minor Hindu deity?

Jehovah's Witnesses

The Jehovah's Witnesses originaterd from a sect originally called the Russellites founded in 1870. In 1931 the title Jehovah's Witnesses was proclaimed by Joseph Rutherford, the second President of their legal corporation, the Watch Tower Bible and Tract Society.

The Witnesses claim a worldwide membership of over 2 million people. According to one report, 'in 40 countries they are banned from holding assemblies and going from door to door to propagate their faith.' In Ireland they have a membership of about 2,000.

At the present time the Jehovah's Witnesses are going through a particularly turbulent time. One of the major defections from the Witnesses in recent years was a member of the seventeen strong governing body of the organisation from 1971. In Ireland two of the most prominent members of the sect, John May and Martin Merriman, resigned and brought others with them.

Doctrine

According to Witness doctrine there is but one God who is called Jehovah. They condemn the Trinity as pagan idolatry and they consequently deny the divinity of Christ. They consider Jesus to be the greatest of Jehovah's Witnesses. He died as a man and was raised as an immortal spirit Son. His passion and death were the price he paid to regain for mankind the right to live eternally on earth. Russell predicted that Armageddon, the final end of the world, would happen before 1914. The date has been revised on a number of occasions. The Witnesses are deeply convinced that the end of the world will come within a few years.

There is an obligation on every Jehovah's Witness to propagate their doctrines. Preaching the 'good news' is the only means of salvation. They do not believe in sacraments. They hold a memorial of the Last Supper once a year. They are opposed to blood transfusions even when there would appear to be a danger of death. The idea of hell is rejected, because they hold that a loving God cannot torment people for ever.

Because of their insistence on offensive convert-making tactics (the ordinary Witness must give ten hours monthly to this work), the Jehovah's Witnesses can be very objectionable. They are persistent and dogmatic. They use and accept the Bible but interpret it to fit their own doctrinal beliefs.

Once a person leaves the organisation, members are forbidden to have any further contact with them. Former members are regarded as apostates. There was serious controversy over this practice in 1983 among the witnesses in Ireland.

School of Philosophy & Economic Science

This organisation might seem out of place among the 'New Elect'. However, there are many unanswered questions about the School. It appears, at least on the surface, to sell counterfeit goods. The School advertises extensively and invites 'those seeking an understanding of human existence and the world in which man lives' to enroll for a twelve-lecture course at the Irish headquarters at 65 Lower Baggot Street, Dublin 2. A brochure introducing the course explains that 'the sense in which the word economics is used in the School is that it refers to the laws governing the household of human society'. It further claims that 'not being associated with political, religious, or sectional interests, the School invites students in the course to be free to join in examining afresh some of the questions which face mankind in the field of economics'.

The extraordinary feature of an organisation using the title 'School of Philosophy and Ecomonic Science' is that none of the courses study standard works of any of the major economists or philosophers. I spoke to the Anglican Bishop of Woolwich, Rt Rev. Michael Marshall, who first condemned this organisation. He maintained that 'it is an insidious organisation. They are power maniacs and really do want to manipulate people's lives. They are a society with spiritual aims that have gone wrong.'

The students and ex-students I spoke to confirmed 'that lectures were read from notes, none of the lecturers had degrees or teaching qualifications, students were not encouraged to ask questions'. Each class begins with meditation to help relaxation.

Like TM there is a ceremony of initiation for those who take the more advanced class. Advanced students learn to read and study Sanskrit. Certain types of diet are encouraged. Students are encouraged to get deeply involved in the maintenance of the school — cleaning, baking, arranging flowers. This despite the fact that there is a fee of £25 for the lecture course.

An article in the *Irish Independent* (24 May 1983) claimed that 'a common pattern reported is its withdrawal from society, rejection of anyone outside the philosophy group, refusal to discuss the ideas involved and increasing dependence on the organisation'.

One person familiar with the group wrote to me explaining that 'my own impression was that the people who took their various courses were reasonably well-off, spiritually confused and looking for something "new" to try. I found it hard to object to a few people relieving them of some money in exchange for a rather undemanding humanism which, as your literature shows, is hermetically sealed to the divine.'

An article in *The Standard* (23 August 1983) claimed that the School's 'ideas are a mixture of philosophy and religion culled from many ancient teachings'.

I include The School of Philosophy and Economic Science not because I consider it a danger but because of its deceptive advertisements and the concealment of its religious dimension.

The Church of Jesus Christ of the Latter-Day Saints (Mormons)

'Mormon' is a nickname for the Church of Jesus Christ of the Latter-Day Saints. In the nineteenth century those who professed belief in the Book of Mormon came to be called Mormons.

Mormons are generally classed as Protestants, but they claim to be 'no closer to Protestantism than to Catholicism'. Neither historically nor on the basis of modern association, theology or practice can they be grouped with either.

The origins of the Church go back to the early nineteenth century when God and Jesus Christ are said to have appeared to fourteen year old Joseph Smith near his home at Palmyra, New York, and told him that all the creeds of current religions were an abomination in their sight. Some years later, in 1830, after further apparitions from an angel called Moroni, Smith founded a church with six members. When he was shot in Illinois, his followers were led south by Brigham Young to Utah and the shores of the great Salt Lake, where his successors have been ever since.

Every boy over twelve may be a priest in the Mormon Church. There are two orders of priesthood, Aaronic and Melchizedek. The Aaronic is concerned with the temporal affairs of the church, the Melchizedek is principally concerned with spiritual affairs. Within each order there are various grades.

Mormonism claims to be a modern revelation of old principles, divinely pronounced with new emphasis and completeness in our day. They believe that many errors have crept into the Bible because of the manner in which the book has come to us. Supplementing the Bible, the Mormons have three other books known as: 'The Book of Mormon', 'The Doctrine and Covenants' and 'The Pearl of Great Price'.

The Church of Jesus Christ of the Latter-Day Saints claims to be God's true Church on earth. They believe the Bible to be the Word of God in so far as it is translated correctly. The Book of Mormon claims that a correct translation of the Bible is impossible since the Catholic Church has taken away from the Word of God many parts which are plain and most precious; and also many converts of the Lord have been taken away.'

The ancient law of the 'tithe' is the financial law of the Church. Latter-Day Saints believe and accept it as being of divine pronouncement. Each member is expected to contribute one-tenth of his income to the Church.

Marriage in Mormon theology is a sacred contract, divinely ordained. Under the authority of the priesthood a man and a women are married not only for life, but for eternity. Such a marriage takes place in a sacred temple of which there are only thirteen in use in the Church, and it is performed only by the few men with authority to do so.

The number of Mormons in Ireland has doubled since 1973 according to District President, Bartholomew Ball. He estimates that of the thousand members in the Republic 95 per cent are former practising Catholics. The Church, which claims to be the fastest growing church in the world in terms of membership, has around one hundred full-time missionaries in Ireland. The Mormons have three churches in the Republic of Ireland.

The Children of God

America, the land of revivalism, has from the start alternated between its view of an awesome Christ and an accessible Christ. The Children of God was spawned from the counter-culture of the late 1960's when God was hijacked by the 'Jesus freaks'. An age when reflection and theology was always subservient to experience, the Age of Aquarius.

The group was started through a 'coffee house' ministry headed by a former minister of the Christian Missionary Alliance Church, David Berg. Berg gathered a following of young people around him. In 1969 he became convinced that a great earthquake was imminent and he left California with his followers and made for Arizona. The Children of God became one of many groups who believe that a long trail of disasters in the world presages the imminent return to earth of Jesus Christ. Berg and his followers take biblical names. Berg took the name Moses — shortened to 'Mo'.

In the beginning the Children of God held a fairly orthodox fundamentalist evangelical brand of Christianity. The group practised austerity. A common feature of the Children of God has been its consistent opposition to the main-line Christian Churches. Berg has always kept a very tight control on the group's activities. This was done through a regular newsletter entitled 'The Letters of Mo'. This letter, giving Berg's latest thoughts, has always been eagerly digested by his followers. The group expanded rapidly and was established in Ireland in the early 1970s. The young people lived together. At one time they had a house in Drumcondra. They lived an austere life. Much of their time was spent evangelising in the city centre or at the airport. *Time* called them 'the storm troopers of the Jesus Revolution'.

Under the influence of Berg the Children of God have strayed more and more from the central truths of Christianity. Richard Cottrell, European MP for Bristol, in a report to the European Parliament, singled out the Children of God, also known as the Family of Love, as 'a threat which governments are not taking seriously enough'.

It is claimed that the women of the Children of God are taught to go to smart night spots and seduce men either to raise money or to recruit them; a method they call 'flirty fishing'. A report in the London *Times* claimed that unmarried women of the group are encouraged, and paid, to bear 'Jesus babies' for the group. This strategy of the use of sex is confirmed by Berg himself: 'when all other avenues of influence and witnessing are closed to us this may be our only remaining means of spreading the Word and supporting the work, as well as gaining new disciples and workers for the Kingdom of God'.

Like other world-rejecting movements the Children of God, through its leader, demands a very high level of self-abnegation. The individual is always subordinate to the group. The well-being of the movement is paramount. A high sense of group solidarity is generated. This facilitates obedience and it is always a very effective deterrent against leaving the group. To leave it is to have failed.

The Children of God or the Family of Love have become diffuse over the years. They no longer have regular meetings or a colony in Dublin. However they are often active in the most popular continental holiday locations. Young Irish people have been contacted and recruited abroad. The movement tended to attract young people who were confused and uncertain and not likely to succeed in a fiercely competitive world. I would imagine that many seemingly well-motivated young people joined as an escape route from the tedium of seeking to make their own way in the world.

Rajneeshism

Of all the new religious groups to hit the Western world the most esoteric must surely be that of Bhagwan Shree Rajneesh. To his followers Bhagwan is an enlightened spiritual master. He is to them 'a Jesus, a Buddha, a Krishna'. He was born in the State of Madhya Pradesh in India in 1931. In common with so many of the founders of new religious groups, Bhagwan became enlightened or 'reborn' at the age of twenty-one. At one time he was a professor of philosophy at the University of Jabalpur. In 1969 he was invited to speak at the Second World Conference on Hindu Religion. He used the opportunity to lash out at organised religion, priests and the hypocrisy of religion. In 1970 he introduced 'dynamic meditations'. He built up a group of disciples in Bombay. In 1974 he moved, because of his health, to Poona where a six-acre property was given to him. It was at Poona that he came to world-wide attention.

Doctrine
The Ashram at Poona was a place where everything was accepted and nothing prohibited. It was combination of bioenergetics, Gestalt therapy, primal therapy with a forceful emphasis on sexual 'liberation'. Bhagwan has been described as a sex guru. The Ashram attracted up to 30,000 people each year, 'predominantly middle-class, well-educated and young'. Every evening Bhagwan held 'darshans' in which he gave initiation and gave new names to disciples. One commentator writes: 'to attempt to describe Bhagwan's teaching is asking for trouble.... Bhagwan himself illustrates the point by saying that he is 'inconsistently inconsistent'.[5]

There are three stages in the Bhagwan's teaching:

(a) The recognition of the Master and surrender to him as a disciple.

(b) Extending that recognition to the community of disciples that has grown up around the Master and seeing the beauty in oneself and in other disciples. This is the Buddhafield- a sharing of energies and a harmonious integration between disciples.

(c) The experience of truth that is directly available in every moment of life, and its joys accepted.

Sanyasim (followers) wear red, purple or orange clothes and have a Sanskrit name. Their 'worship' takes the form of Sufi dancing, formalised jumping and shouting, and silence.

In 1981 Bhagwan ceased speaking, left India and set up headquarters at the Rajneesh Foundation International in Oregon on an enormous cattle ranch. Like other new 'pseudo-religious' groups money does not seem to be a problem. Bhagwan himself drives around the huge ranch estate in one of the many Rolls Royces given to him by devoted followers.

Baha'ism

Aims to establish a unity of the human race, of all religions, and of science, and advocates universal education, world peace through social equality and opposition to all forms of prejudice, equal rights for the sexes, an international language and an international tribunal.

This religion was founded by Baha'Ullah (the splendour of God) who was born in Tehran in 1817. According to Baha'i tradition he received no formal education. In 1983 Baha'Ullah declared his prophethood and sent letters to various sovereigns inviting them to accept Baha'ism.

Baha'ism propounds a body of doctrine that clearly originated in Shiite Islam but closely resembles Unitarianism. It is syncretistic and universalist. The Baha'i faith, which claims to have 2 million members in 173 countries has no clergy as such. They maintain that Moses, Zoroaster, Buddha, Christ, Mohammed and Baha'Ullah were all 'divine educators' on mankind's route to enlightenment. (Muslims regard this as a terrible heresy, since they believe that Mohammed was the last of the prophets.) Their religion forbids them to take part in politics and they firmly believe in female emancipation.

Almost since their inception the Baha'is have been persecuted in Persia. It happened in the early part of the Shah's reign, when he wanted to appease the Muslim clerics. During the rule of Khomeini in Iran the Baha'is have been persecuted. About 271 are in jail and over 140 have been executed. The Baha'is have a growing community in Ireland.

The EST Training

According to the EST Training brochure it is an 'educational and philosophical enquiry into three aspects of life; knowing, reality and creation. The training is about an expansion of those activities and aspirations which we held clearly when we were growing up, and which we may have put aside or given up in the daily process of living our lives. It is about rediscovering the power we inherently have, to choose our lives and be able to live from a place of integrity and responsibility.'

The EST training takes two weekends, lasts about sixty hours, and costs £250. There are three additional evening seminars around the training, which are recommended but are not compulsory. Like TM the EST Training makes very extravagant promises — 'people report results in all areas of their lives, in deeper personal relationships, more vitality and an ability to relax and sleep when needed, better health and more co-operation and satisfaction at work'.

EST stands for Erhard Seminars Training after the founder Werner Erhard, or John Paul Rosenberg, as he was formerly known. This is one more group in the human potential movement. It belongs to the 'family' of TM, Silva Mind Control, and some forms of Yoga.

EST is particularly subjective in its interpretation of life. There is no objective truth, no absolutes. One observer of the human potential movement notes that, rather than God, adherents are likely to refer to 'my ground of being, my true nature, the ultimate energy'; and that the common image of God is the notion of cosmic energy as a life force in which all partake'.[17] Erhard has stated, 'For instance, I believe that the belief in God is the greatest barrier to God in this universe — the greatest single barrier. I would prefer someone who is ignorant to someone who believes in God because belief in God is a total barrier, almost a total barrier to the experience of God'. (*East-West Journal*, September 1974)

EST and other similar movements focus on the subjective. The problems of the world can and will be solved by the use of certain techniques. If enough individuals would meditate or chant particular phrases then a change can come about in the world order. The emphasis is always on personal fulfilment. You are or can become your own god and everything you experience, even a bad thing like assault, is a product of your own divine creative will.

The Elim Pentecostal Church

History

Founded in the county of Monaghan, Ireland, in 1915, the movement which came to bear the name 'Elim Foursquare

Gospel Alliance' grew with amazing rapidity. It is included in the great worldwide Pentecostal movement, a movement acclaimed as the fastest-growing Church of the present age.

The name 'Elim' is taken from the Book of Exodus, where we read that the Israelites encamped in the wilderness and refreshed themselves by the wells of water in the shade of palm trees. (*Exodus 15:27*). 'The objects of the Alliance are to spread the full Gospel of our Lord Jesus Christ and the fundamental truths herein set forth'.

Government

The governing body of the Elim Pentecostal Church is the Conference, which is made up of ministers and laymen and which meets annually for business and fellowship. Each church has its board of elders and deacons, who, together with the minister, form the Church Session. These brethren are responsible for the spiritual and financial statement to the annual church meeting. A balance sheet and accounts of the central funds are also published each year by the Elim Headquarters.

An Executive Council is elected from among members of the Conference. It meets quarterly to carry out decisions and conduct the business of the Movement. There are also officers and committees appointed to help the smooth running of the various departments. All Headquarters' officers are voted in by the Conference.

Properties are held in trust for the congregation either by local trustees under the terms of a model trust deed or by the Elim Trust Corporation, a body legally constituted to hold these buildings for the people.

Doctrine

Membership of an Elim Pentecostal Church does not depend on rites or knowledge of creeds, but upon a personal experience of salvation. All who have accepted Jesus Christ as Saviour and Lord and have been born again are eligible as members and can be received into fellowship by the minister at a church meeting. There, are however, certain doctrines to which Elim churches subscribe. Certain ordinances are observed: breaking of bread and drinking of wine in memory of our Lord's death (Holy Communion); baptism by total immersion in water; anointing of the sick with oil for the healing of the body.

NOTES

1. Eileen Barker, 'Some Thoughts on the Unification Church' *The Clergy Review*, October 1980, p. 366.
2. Eileen Barker.
3. *Contemporary Christianity*, vol. 8.2, January 1979.
4. *The Science of Self-Realisation*, The Bhaktivedanta Book Trust.
5. Bob Mullan, *Life as Laughter: following Bhagwan Shree Rajneesh*, Routledge and Kegan Paul, 1983, p. 32.

7

PARENTS AND CULTS

The evangelical zeal of many of the new religious groups that have arrived in Ireland in the past few years has borne considerable fruit in terms of new converts gained. This has naturally been a cause of great pain and anxiety to the parents of these young people. I understand their pain. The response on the part of parents has often been to level serious accusations of wrongdoing against the groups or to become involved in a public crusade against their activities. This is often a response born out of frustration and an inability to cope with the situation.

Over the past ten years I have had the opportunity of meeting and speaking with many members and ex-members of what are popularly known as 'cults'. I believe that there are certain personality features common to the recruits to the new groups that are worth noting.

1. Many are of the 'seeker individual' category. They have found that the traditional faith in which they were reared no longer fulfils a felt need within them. They are searching, often without knowing it. Such individuals will occasionally move from one group to another until they find a degree of spiritual and emotional stability which anchors them with one group. I noted that many of those who came to the Charismatic Renewal did so after trying TM, EST or some form of growth therapy. In the same way I have met individuals in the Hare Krishna and The Way International who had arrived in these movements, having tried Charismatic Renewal. Indeed, some seem to be on a continual pilgrimage from one group to the other. Each group is the 'answer', for the time being at least.

2. The second type of individual who seems drawn to the new groups is the young person who has rejected, in a very definite way, the spirituality and theology of the established churches. They also reject what they see as the hypocrisy of Church leaders and of their own families.

   This type seem attracted by the austerity of life proposed by many of the groups as a way of living. They almost glory in the rigour of their lives. They are prepared to engage in endless fund-raising and 'witnessing', distributing tracts and seeking donations as in the case of the Children of God. Endless prayers and chanting and a very meagre diet are willingly accepted.

   They are unwilling to act out a 'charade' of conformity in order to please their parents. These are young people who allege that the Churches have gone 'soft' and have accommodated themselves totally to the world. They claim that the Church has lost the real spiritual dynamic of the early Church. In two different groups I have met former nuns and a former priest who illustrate this point.

3. A third type is the 'drop out'. However, the individual may not see himself as such. The pressures of life, the competitiveness of the examination system and fear of failure are all reasons for finding a valuable way of life that makes leaving the 'rat race' easy and justifiable. It is difficult for such a person to leave the group once they have joined.

4. An emotional low point in a young person's life can cause him to look for solace or help in an unconventional 'religion'. The break-up of a relationship or serious family difficulties can be a point of decision. On occasion an attempt to break with an addictive habit like drug-taking can lead a young person to seek help from a religious group of which they then become a member.

Parents

Many parents do not know their children. They are often overcome and baffled by the fact that they have joined a new religious group. They immediately galvanise themselves into action without any reflection. Some parents have physically attacked members of the 'cults'. On occasions they have also broken property and done wilful damage. I do not believe that meeting the situation with force is any answer.

My advice to parents is prevention. The building up of a good family life is the surest way of ensuring children's growth into maturity. The faithful relationship between a father and a mother is the primary gift that parents give their child. It has been said that values are caught, not taught: it is in the home that the young person will receive a vision for Christian living that will be a support in times of difficulty. The way that the parents live out their Christian faith will give their children a model of living.

The Pastoral Letter of the Western Bishops in 1980 put it this way: 'The home of believing Christians should never be able to be mistaken for the home of people who have not the faith. Their house should be recognisable and clearly identifiable as a place whose members believe, whose members pray.'[1] This pastoral also emphasises a very important point in relation to giving young people reasons for believing: 'We adults can be copping out if we are not prepared to give our teenage children reasons for what we know to be the deepest truths and truest values which give meaning and worth to our lives and will give meaning to theirs.' The believing home where love is fostered is the very best insurance policy against the possibility of young people being misled into joining a 'new religious group or cult'.

It may be a sad indictment against Christian family life and the Christian Churches that 'many ex-cultists, when discussing the reason for being so deeply affected by the cultic love tactic, noted they had never received the personal love and attention they needed from their families or childhood Churches.'[2]

Beware of Deception

Over the last few years a large number of new evangelical Christian groups, as well as the cults, have begun to operate in this country. Many of them do their utmost to align their public image with the main-line Churches, especially the Catholic Church. One or two of these groups have gone to great lengths to use the media and Catholic periodicals to find an acceptance among Catholic people. Partly because of this, young people are joining 'Bible groups'. Unsuspecting parents, not knowing anything of their nature, often encourage the young person to continue their involvement with the group. I would urge that when it comes to a Bible or prayer group it is important to check out the nature of the group. Get information. Obviously this should be done in a sincere spirit of enquiry. Ask your son or daughter about the group, the type of teaching that is given, who the leaders are, and the format of the meeting. This of course ought to be part of any good relationship between a parent and child. The group can become the subject of genuine conversation.

It is much easier to provide guidance and to point the young person into other Church activities before they become over-committed to a 'new religion'. Once they enter into commitments, even that of attending a weekly meeting, the task of providing good parental guidance within a Church framework becomes much more difficult.

If the young person insists on maintaining contact with an evangelical group make sure that they do not become over-involved. This may mean that they would be permitted to attend only once a week. While children are living at home they do have a responsibility and obligation to respect the wishes of their parents. I think it is important that parents be strict in this matter. All of these groups tend to assign tasks or 'ministries' which have the result of drawing a person into commitments to which they have not given consideration.

If your child has become involved in a cult such as the Hare Krishna, The Divine Light Mission or the Moonies, then a much more serious view must be taken. I would ask them to break the contact, at least temporarily. The next task is to seek information about the group or to enlist the aid of a mature person with pastoral experience who can talk with your child. Many parents might be tempted to consider youthful dabbling with cults as a passing fad. It may indeed pass. However, my experience is that very few return to the practice of their original faith. There is also the possibility that they will be confused and perhaps emotionally disturbed as a result of their experience. Their studies are often seriously interrupted and even their health may be affected.

Church Groups

Sympathy and understanding are important ingredients in maintaining trust and confidence between parents and children. Try to find out what exactly your son or daughter is seeking in the cult. Is it prayer, a community lifestyle, or is it a genuine search for truth? Perhaps the influence of friends has managed to dull your child's critical faculties. Take time to talk and find out exactly what it is they are looking for. It may be possible to demonstrate that their aspirations can be fulfilled within the Church. It is a great advantage to know what is available for young people within the life of the Church. Organisations like the Young Christian Workers, The Focolare, The Peace Corps, the local Church folk groups, and the Taizé Movement are attracting many young people today. There are also community-based organisations that cater for young people — examples of these are Renewal and Youth and The Christian Life Communities. There are also a number of groups that are involved in third world issues which are thus attractive to young people. A listing of such organisations can be found in the Irish Catholic Directory or the Dublin Diocesan Directory which are available in most book stores. Other Christian denominations also have youth groups with a spiritual orientation. When young people say 'the Church is dead' I find that they are simply not aware of what is available to them within the Church.

Try to get your child to think and question for himself. Because of the strong authoritarian nature of the cults and of many of the evangelical sects questioning is discouraged. The emphasis is usually on experience and community. Encourage thinking on the leadership of the group, on the obedience that is expected, and on the fundraising activities. Point to the two thousand year tradition of the Catholic Church. However, don't offer solutions too soon. Listen to his feelings and concerns.

The World and the New Religions

Most of the 'new religious' groups will have prepared new recruits for efforts to detach them from the group. A first step in this preparation will be prayer for the conversion of parents and family. Strategies for family conversation will be discussed. The implication of all this is to present a simplistic interpretation of religious life in black and white, saved or not saved. The parents, as long as they remain unconvinced of the authenticity of the group, belong to the world and are therefore under the influence of the evil one, bad karma or whatever terms they use. They will be expecting hostility. A hostile parent is one who is acting true to form. One young cult member asked her mother if she knew she (the mother) was doing the work of Satan?'

Hostility frequently strengthens the resolve of the young person to remain within the group. I am convinced that a hostile approach to anyone who has joined a 'new religion' or cult is counter-productive. That is why I am firmly against so-called deprogramming. Maintain relations on a friendly basis. Parents of my acquaintance have done this with their child and now after a number of years all the indications are that the child is about to leave the group. I have a reasonable expectation that there will be an integrated return to family life. It is unlikely that this would have happened if the parents had rejected their child in the begining.

Do not antagonise the leaders of the cults. By all means discuss the future of your child with the leader but make sure to keep the lines of communication open at all times. Insist that your child be allowed to complete her education. Ask for a definite commitment on this.

If your child has left home to live in a communal situation try to ensure that she will be allowed home on a regular basis. These visits ought to include overnight stays. If she does come home encourage him to renew acquaintance with her former friends. Discuss the ordinary events of family life. Do not change family patterns because the young person is home, particularly in the area of family prayer or other religious activity. It is better not to use the occasion to launch an attack on the group. Discuss the group if it fits naturally into the pattern of family conversation. This is a time when restraint and patience are required as never before.

Adult Religious Education

An important step in helping young people who have got caught up in pseudo-religious groups is to know your own Church. Learn something of its traditions, doctrine and history. Young people learn rapidly. As soon as they join a cult or an evangelical sect they are immediately put to learning and studying the theology and 'spirituality' of the group. They gain a superficial facility in answering the commonest objections to the group and its doctrine. This is one of the reasons why Catholics who join evangelical groups cease sacramental practice within a short time. It is not so much that the Church is attacked directly but rather that because of the nature of the teaching it is shown to be irrelevant. Most parents ought to be able to have a reasonable conversation on a religious topic with their children. Find a good book on Catholic doctrine to read or study. Enrol in an adult education course in religion that will equip you to converse with your children.

Seek Professional Help

Over the years I have had occasion to visit the casualties of the cults and of some evangelical sects in psychiatric hospitals. Some of the more evangelical groups place a great emphasis on the ministry of 'deliverance'. By this is meant exorcising an individual from possession by the devil or evil spirits. A person of a very sensitive nature or one who is already suffering mentally could be damaged. Such people are also more open to manipulation. If you have a child of a very sensitive nature then special care ought to be taken with their religious upbringing.

Snapping

The heightened atmosphere generated at meetings of cults and some pentecostal groups can be upsetting to some people, especially those who are already disturbed. Something can be triggered off in a person who otherwise appears normal. I believe that involvement in a highly charged atmosphere can be the occasion for 'snapping' but I am less sure that it is the cause. Conway and Siegelman write, in *Snapping*,[3] 'in the wake of snapping, after an individual surrenders, "lets go", whether in a sudden moment or gradually, he may possibly slip into a level of reduced awareness in which the disorientation and confusion that follows the snapping moment becomes part of his everyday manner of experiencing the world. This trance-like limbo state represents the suspension of a person's response as an individual and is the first stage in the reorganisation of personality.' It is important to be on the alert for significant changes of personality, mood, or values. If these changes are prolonged and include peculiar behaviour patterns there may be reason to seek competent professional help.

Fundraising

Many of the better-known cults spend much of their time fundraising. Parents will be approached for funds. Don't give money either to the group in which your child is involved or to your child personally. Giving financial aid, apart from the fact that you are helping some spurious group to flourish, may prolong your child's involvement with the group. Much of the money collected may go out of the country. It will also be used to support full-time members of the group.

Conversion

There are genuine conversions to evangelical groups and to cults. Parents and others point to personality changes as evidence of the transitory nature of the involvement, as proof of 'brainwashing' or psychological manipulation. But people do change their religion. Sometimes the signs are wrongly interpreted. Conversion experiences can be transforming. People can act differently and think differently as a result of deep religious commitment. Many groups actually deliver what they promise in the form of 'a meaningful interpretation of life, a sense of bondedness or social fellowship, experiences of transcendence, and a strict code of behaviour to follow'.[4]

Sad though it may be for Roman Catholic parents to accept, an increasing number of young people are not just going to lapse, but are going to transfer their allegiance to other denominations, evangelical groups or cults. It is in cases like this that tolerance, faith and patience are required.

Parents ought to make their own religious convictions clear, their attitude should be unambiguous. They should seek to maintain the family bonds of love. Silence may be interpreted as tolerance, hostility may sever relationships irrevocably. The path to be mapped out is that of love.

Churchification

Hopefully parents will read this book. A word of consolation. Not all young people who continue to go to Church are evangelised in the sense of having a personal relationship with Jesus Christ. In the fifth century St Augustine warned about conforming without interior transformation.

Putting your son or daughter 'back on the rolls' may not be a solution to their problem. The search for something to stand for may mean a painful stepping aside from the mainstream ideology of their peer group. There are times when I have been edified by the sacrifices the young people in cults have made to live out their new beliefs. Nobody looks for continuing hassle with parents, school, friends. Life inside most of the 'world rejecting' cults is austere. A very high level of self-sacrifice is demanded of the young people. Monotony and boredom with ceaseless fundraising, chanting, distributing literature calls for a degree of commitment that would be difficult to expect from main-line Christians.

If very close, warm contact is maintained with the young cultist there must be the possibility of a return to the Church and a renewal of a personal relationship with Jesus Christ. Their generosity can eventually be channelled into the mission of the Church.

Priests

Young people need time to talk out their fears as well as their convictions. It is possible for priests to maintain friendly relations with those who have left the Church. I have never been refused admission to speak or pray with evangelicals or cult members. I have always been made welcome. Even though it is known that a priest is in opposition to their beliefs and practices, if he demonstrates a willingness to listen and try to understand this will always be appreciated.

Priests need to be informed, not necessarily to provide the immediate ready answer, but to assist the young people in their search for the truth which we believe has been revealed in Jesus Christ.

Even when young people leave cults or groups they still need to have the opportunity to sort things out. Leaving the group is not the end of the problem. Some leave and then rejoin before being able to make the final break. Others leave and then begin to drift aimlessly. Young people who leave as intense an experience as is embodied in many cults need continuing pastoral care. There are difficulties in adjusting to life outside the warmth of the group. These difficulties must be understood by priests and parents.

'Overwhelming moods of depression and loneliness often arise. Former members realise and regret the fact that they are out of step both in their working and social worlds. Some feel abused by their cult experience. Because cults restrict all physical experience and contact, many ex-members also have intimacy and sexual growth difficulties. And leaving a cult means leaving behind loved ones — comrades who have shared a special experience with you. Former members must quickly find new friends in a world that they have been led to believe is hostile.'[5]

Forming good friendships can be a real help to the person who has managed to leave a cult. Here a Church group which is not too aggressively evangelical can assist. The young person must be given the 'space' to work on his own religious convictions. Help should be available but not forced on the young person. But they must know that it is available. I have met a number of young ex-cultists who have continued to drift aimlessly simply because the right kind of help was not offered.

It is unlikely that a young person who has left a cult will return to the Church immediately. The reason for leaving the cult in the first place may have been a growing disillusionment with all religion. Problems with authority within the group may be another reason for leaving. It is unrealistic to expect a return to a Church which also places a high premium on obedience to spiritual authority. The young person must be encouraged to make mature personal and responsible decisions for his or her own life. This is a matter that may take some time. Be prepared to give time.

NOTES

1. *Handing on the Faith in the Home*, Irish Catholic Bishops' Conference, Veritas, 1980.
2. Daniel C. Markham, *Cults and Cultism* (Unpublished manuscript).
3. Conway & Siegelman *Snapping*, Delta Books, 1978, p. 155.
4. *Cults and Sects - An Assessment* - Richard Wood OP, NCR Cassettes.
5. Robert Dellinger, *Cults and Kids*, Boys' Town Centre

8

THE CHURCH AND YOUTH

Do the new religious groups and the cults present a real threat to the major Christian churches in Ireland? In terms of numbers the answer is no. Roy Wallis, in his excellent book, *Elementary Forms of the New Religious Life,*[1] concludes that the new religious movements have made little impression on the drift from the Christian Churches. The new groups are picking up very few recruits from those young people who are ceasing to believe in and practise their Christian faith. He instances the drift from the Protestant Churches in Britain, claiming that 'Protestant Churches in Britain lost over half a million members between 1970 and 1975 alone, during which time the conservative churches that were growing gained about 14,000 new members, making no impression on the overall decline. In 1975, less than 20 per cent of the United Kingdom claimed Church membership, leaving approximately 34 million adults available for recruitment to new religious groups. In these circumstances the suggestion that the new religious movements — with for example, 588 resident British Moonies in 1980 or 536 British Children of God in 1981 are an effective response, making an impact upon the substantial unchurched, is scarcely compelling.'[6]

I believe that the Irish experience is the same as that cited in Britain. It is very difficult to obtain information on the actual numbers involved in the better-known cults such as the Moonies or the Children of God. Some of these groups keep changing address. When asked about the numbers involved the answers are usually evasive or, where an actual number is given, I suspect that it is inflated. Some groups have degrees of membership, so that associates are sometimes included in these membership figures.

Groups come and go and then come again. The Children of God, for instance were quite strong in the early 1970s after which they disappeared completely. I have recently heard of their return. The same is true of the Divine Light Mission who tried to make a comeback with a rally in the National Concert Hall in Dublin. The Hare Krishna have been strong in recent years but they are now considering leaving their Dublin temple and going to the North of Ireland. The Way International has steadily been gaining ground. This may be because the leadership here is completely Irish and is able to identify closely with young people. Again, their period of decline may be close at hand as the 'revolving door' syndrome saps the morale of the leaders and members. Only a few people manage to persevere with most of these movements and this tends to weaken the resolve of the remainder to continue the way of life.

The groups that are increasing their numbers of adherents are the fundamentalist evangelical Christian groups, The Mormons, Transcendental Meditation, The School of Philosophy and Economic Science, the House Church Movement.

The media have always tended to focus on the more bizarre groups. The impression was given that they were more numerous than they actually were. There has been a great deal of unhelpful publicity which has put the emphasis on combatting the cults rather than pastoring those who are leaving the Church or are disillusioned by it. I agree that there is a ministry, and an important one, to cultists and their parents and families. However the publicity could lead pastors up a sterile cul-de-sac. The real problem in the Church in Ireland today is not the activity of the cults but the failure of the Church to develop a real evangelical outreach to many of our young people.

The Lessons to be Learned

Is there anything to be learned from the growth of new religious groups in Ireland? We must remember that they are dealing with a homogeneous group of people, namely the young. The Church has a ministry to all ages and classes.

The problem is not in the message but in the appropriation of the message. Proclamation is only one dimension of the mission of the Church. How does the message enter the bloodstream of the Church's life? In my contacts with the cults and evangelical Christian groups what impressed me most was the system of teaching and pastoring that they had invariably developed. They assisted the young people into a new way of living. All the groups that I have written about in this book pay particular attention to teaching and to the appropriation of the message that they wish to convey, for example there is detailed teaching on how to overcome temptation in the areas of sexuality and justice, and speeches are given regularly. They were convinced that it isn't enough to say that something is wrong but that it is also necessary to demonstrate that it is possible to live up to the teaching that is given. Progress is monitored by mutual consent and on an ongoing basis. This is as true of the Hare Krishna as it is of the evangelical groups. The growing moral confusion in the Church can only be untangled by clear teaching and gentle, firm and, if possible, personal pastoring.

The second important aspect of the new groups is that they offer a real challenge to young people. They are not afraid to make demands on them. The Mormons demand 10 per cent of the income of all their followers. The Jehovah's Witnesses give one year of their lives to unpaid voluntary missionary work. The Hare Krishna eschew alcohol, meat, sex, and tobacco. They all believe the truth of what they preach and they claim that the appropriation of the 'truth' will demand sacrifice. I know what you are thinking — 'sure doesn't the Church do the same'. But there is the world of difference between pastoral letters which are read from the altar, or papal statements heard over the media and a challenge personally presented. The demands have to be presented within the context of the overall message and somehow in a more personal way. Here of course I am speaking of those who have already left school and are not in a position to receive the message personally unless they belong to some apostolic group. The basic Christian communities of the Latin American Church are impressive in that the message is presented in a challenging personal way. I recall being very impressed on entering a large church hall in Sao Paulo where about twenty groups of young people were studying Christian doctrine — and not a priest in sight!

Thirdly, the evangelical zeal of the new religious groups is impressive. They are out on the streets, in the universities, attending the annual 'pop' festivals. They are constantly on the look-out for new recruits. I imagine that the average diocesan priest in Ireland spends the major part of his daily schedule with the converted. Not so with the cults or the evangelicals! Attention and care for the material fabric of the Church's plant is important. But plant without people is not Church! The Church now has to be brought to the people. For a long time we have taken it for granted that the traffic would always be the other way around. It is here that I make a plea for the Church to place more of its resources at the disposal of some scheme for the retraining of priests and selected lay people in youth ministry and evangelisation. We priests, particularly those over forty, have been trained to minister to a believing Church. The emphasis was, and rightly so, on the ministry of the sacraments. This work must of course continue. But meanwhile there is a need to minister to those who have strayed. I believe that this is a special ministry. It is interesting that The Way International has the wherewithal to send personnel to the US on a regular basis to be trained. We certainly can learn something from the crusading zeal of the new religious groups. Don't get me wrong — I am not advocating aggressive flag-waving evangelism. However the situation has so changed in Ireland over the last twenty years that the pastoral methodology of the past needs serious re-thinking.

A fourth aspect of the new religious groups that we can learn from is in the area of community building. Community is a hackneyed word. It applies to everything from the EEC to the local community council. In the area of religious groups it has the very specific meaning of teaching and instructing people to relate in a committed and ongoing way as brothers and sisters in the Lord. Many people argue that the future hope for the Church lies in building and strengthening small groups of committed Christians who will act as a leaven in society. There has been a 'community boom' in evangelical Christianity. Other non-Christian groups often derive their strength and their ability to persevere from the living out of close brotherly relationships. The extraordinary success of the House Church movement, particularly in England, is an illustration of how the building of community can affect the life of a Church for good or ill.

Building Christian community is a particular pastoral skill. It will make great demands and sacrifices on those who decide to embark on this course. No Christian community is built on 'cheap grace'. It is difficult to live out the Christian life in isolation. This is particularly true of young people. Indeed we all need the support and encouragement of other brothers and sisters if we are to persevere and grow in holiness. That is why we need community, not as an optional extra, but as an important part of living an authentic Christian life. In the future the building of Christian communities, which are open to the world, will be a priority.

A final lesson the Church might learn from the new religious groups is in the area of communication. I have received literature and audio and visual tapes of a very high standard of presentation from many of the new groups. In contrast to the dreary way in which papal encyclicals and pastoral letters are printed and published their literature is impressive. The public have become used to the skilful and sophisticated presentation of a bewildering number of messages from the professional media people. Commitment of a high order is demanded of those who might feel inclined to read Church documents which are clumsily and shoddily presented. In this regard it is important to note that much of the literature presented by new religious groups is geared to the potential recruit. So much of what the Church publishes is 'for the club' — those already committed. I was impressed by the presentation of Church documentation in Brazil. I saw *Laborem Exercens* published in comic form, in the form of a film strip, in cartoon format, and in the printed word. Thus there was a possibility of the message reaching even the illiterate.

Conclusion
Much of what is peddled as genuine religion by many new

religious groups is little more than navel gazing. It encourages an unhealthy form of narcissism. This is particularly true of the 'Human Potential Movement', as Christopher Lash wrote in *The New York Review of Books* (30 September 1976).

A growing despair of changing society — even of understanding it — has generated on the one hand a revival of old-time religion, on the other a cult of expanded consciousness, health, and personal 'growth'. Having no hope of improving their lives in any of the ways that matter, people have convinced themselves that what matters is psychic self-improvement; getting in touch with their feelings, eating health food, taking lessons in ballet or belly dancing, immersing themselves in the wisdom of the East, jogging, learning how to relate, overcoming the fear of pleasure. Harmless in themselves, these pursuits, elevated to a programme and wrapped in the rhetoric of 'authenticity' and 'awareness' signify a retreat from the political turmoil of the recent past. Indeed Americans seem to wish to forget not only the 1960s, the riots, the New Left, the disruption of college campuses, Vietnam, Watergate, and the Nixon presidency, but their entire collective past, even in the antiseptic form of the Bicentennial.

Personal 'fulfilment' has become a goal in itself. If something helps you to feel better then it must be good. This is also an attempt to eliminate all pain from life. Many of the groups in the Human Potential Movement claim to produce instant results. Gullible young people are easily parted from their money, in exchange for a transitory experience of wellbeing. Some may be helpful for a time but ultimately the *agere contra* must be faced and used to purify one in the service of the Lord.

'When you come to serve the Lord prepare yourself for trial' says the Book of Sirach. There is no 'cheap grace' as Bonhoffer pointed out in his book, *The Cost of Discipleship.* To my mind groups that promise immediate gratification even under the guise of spirituality are generally suspect. There are few short cuts to heaven.

There has been a lack of solid and genuine spiritual direction in the Church in recent years. Spiritual masters are needed. People are looking for guidance. This is where I make a special plea for 'pastoring' —which is a new word for the same thing. A spirit of activism has frequently squeezed out the often tedious task of providing mature guidance, in the confessional or elsewhere. One of the reasons that young people are finding value in many of the evangelical groups is that spiritual guidance on a personal level is provided. The Church has the wisdom of the ages at her disposal. It is ironic that thousands of people are discovering the value of meditation from gurus of doubtful authenticity when the West already has the riches of Benedictine and Ignatian prayer. Now is the time to draw on the riches of the Church's spiritual wisdom and to present it to young people. An evangelical Christian preacher was interviewed on television recently. He was invited to counter the accusations made against him that he was encouraging people to leave their Churches and join his group. He replied 'I am not a sheep stealer, but I grow grass'. Perhaps there is a lesson to be learned from his reply.

Appendix 1

WESTERN BISHOPS' LENTEN PASTORAL 1983

RENEWING OUR FAITH IN THE CHURCH

New 'Missions'

For many years we in Ireland took the Church for granted. There was no great challenge to our faith. In recent times however, in some parishes of the West of Ireland, groups from non-Christian and non-Catholic religions have initiated 'missions'. Some non-denominational Christian groups have established themselves in different centres and some groups have broken away from the Catholic Church to set up little 'house-churches' of their own.

Unhappy Consequences

We hear now and again that someone has joined this group or that. Or people we know very well, or even members of our own family, tell us they no longer belong to the Catholic Church. In many cases they begin to seem like different people and they are different. It isn't just that they drop out of being part of the Church, they drop out of being part of the family. Gradually their lives are taken over, their time, their thoughts, their attitudes. They are told what to think and what to say. They attach themselves singlemindedly to certain bits of the Bible that they claim support their beliefs. They depend more and more on the little group that thinks for them and like them. They see the rest of the people as cut off from God. They suspect the rest of the world and see it as hostile. They separate more and more from their friends and family. Even conversation with them can become difficult or strained. Eyes are closed to the good in others, blame is attached to every outsider, but especially to parents, teachers, the Church. They are no longer the boys or girls we knew or loved. They are no longer ours, they are no longer even their own. They have been, not so much converted as taken over.

Questions to be faced

In face of this situation certain questions must be asked:

i) What can we learn from what is happening?

ii) In what way are these groups wrong?

iii) What is the real meaning of the Church, its mission and its place in our lives?

Mission of Church

The Church exists not because man believes in God but because God believes in man. So, because of our need and his love He sent his Son, Jesus Christ, to the earth to be one of us, to help us, to strengthen us, to show us the way, to teach us the truth about our past, our present, our future. He sent Jesus at a particular time in the world's history, but He arranged that Jesus would remain present in the world even after his span of human life on the earth was over. He did this because He loved all people and He knew the people of every generation would need his help, his light. And Jesus, to achieve this presence and to continue his work of salvation through the ages, founded the Church. The purpose of his Church is to do exactly what our Lord came on earth to do — to make Him available to us and to bring us to Him. How was the Church to do this? In two ways: firstly, by preserving and teaching the truth Christ came to reveal — the information about God and us and the world we live in. Secondly, by making Jesus present to us in the ways He himself set up and gave to the Church — the Mass and the Sacraments.

The Church and Scripture

The role of the Church as preserver and teacher of revealed truth is particularly important when we are dealing with Scripture. Random quotations from the Bible, especially when they are taken out of context, can confuse and mislead. It may help you to recall that in the early days of the Church the message of salvation was handed on by word of mouth. When the Gospels came to be written for instance, they weren't just the personal recollections of the four evangelists. They were the work of the entire believing community as well. They were a work of interpretation under the guidance of the Holy Spirit. The Gospels didn't emerge independently of the Church. They were part of her wider preaching tradition. The point to remember is that they still are.

Individual texts or passages have to be understood within the unity of all scripture and the living tradition of the Church. To separate the Scriptures from the Church is to forget their origins and distort their meaning. It is helpful to remember, too, that the authentic interpretation of God's word, whether written or oral, had been entrusted by Jesus Christ to the teaching office in the Church: 'Go, therefore, teach ye all nations. Teach them to observe all the commands I gave you. And know that I am with you always, yes to the end of time' Matt 28: 19-20. This teaching authority in the Church isn't above the word of God but does serve it. It listens to it devoutly, guards it scrupulously and explains it faithfully with the help of the Holy Spirit (Vat. II Divine Rev. Para. 9,10). So never be put out by texts of Scripture quoted at you. Our understanding of Scripture is firmly rooted in the teaching tradition of the Church. The Scripures came from the Church. They remain within it.

Mass and Sacraments

The Church makes Christ available to us and brings us to Him. Not just through his word but by actions and situations too. This is something Christ arranged himself. He wanted to be part of our story so He became a human being like us. He wants us to be part of his story so he gives us the Mass and the Sacraments. You see the Mass and Sacraments are not accidental. They are God's way of breaking through to us in the person of his Son Jesus Christ. He does this at special times in our lives, like Baptism or Marriage and He does it constantly in the special action we call Mass and Eucharist. He wants in the everyday signs of food and drink to share our lives and to link our lives to his great sign of love for us, his death on the Cross. He is our God and we are his people and the Church which brings us the care, the love, the mercy, the healing of Christ is God's way of saying that.

Church as Guide

So that is the reason for the Church — it is God's way of bringing us safely through life to Himself. Now today people sometimes forget, or feel they do not need, the Church. They feel they can settle affairs directly with God without involving the Church as an intermediary or a guide. But then when you think of it, it involves them in contradictions — to believe in God and to reject the ways and means He chose to give us is strange; and is it possible to believe in Christ and to reject what he did and gave? 'Anyone who rejects you rejects me'

Luke 10:16. Our Lord established a Church. Wouldn't it be odd to express belief in Him but not in it? And if you can pick and choose, accepting the bits of Christ's teaching that you like and rejecting what you don't like then you're really founding your own religion, establishing your own church. It may resemble Christ's but it is not his.

Danger of Cults

Even though people who advance the claims of new religious groups are sometimes of the highest calibre, it is unfortunately true that some of the better-known cults can be a great danger to young minds. In their methods of recruitment and in the techniques by which they exercise power over people they are often manipulating and taking advantage of them. In the unfounded doctrines some of them profess, they lead people astray. The end result can be disturbed and disorientated minds. One has only to recall the mass suicide of the members of a particular cult in Guyana some years ago. In a fervent separatist group, young or insecure persons can be robbed of personality and made dependent members. Their immaturity is deepened, their free will compromised and they are separated from the natural, sustaining forces of family and friends.

Signs of Danger

So that are the signs by which one recognises danger?

i) If they give a picture of God that is very different from the loving, forgiving person who created us.

ii) If they demand abject veneration for a human leader or suggest that he may be divine.

iii) If they use the Bible to reject the Church.

iv) If they make salvation the privilege of the very few — themselves — and see all others as unredeemed and lost.

v) If as a result of contact with a group, hitherto open and honest young people become deceitful, secretive and evasive, especially with their own families.

A Challenge

What have we to learn from all this? Perhaps the very presence and growth of these groups are signs to us in the Church; indications of needs to which we do not minister. They hint at a spiritual hunger among some of our people that is often unrecognised. What the cults apparently give to some of their adherents is a sense of belonging, an experience of 'Church' which is markedly at variance with what they might dismissively describe as 'Sunday Catholicism'. The best of what they experience outside the Church must be provided more widely within. If the temper of the times is for the companionship of small groups, the challenge to us is to expand and encourage such groups within the community of the Church. May we all face that challenge courageously in the days ahead.

Sympathy and Concern

This letter is written with great sympathy for those who have experienced this problem. We know that people have been upset, worried, disturbed and saddened by the separation caused even in their own families when a child or brother or sister proclaimed that they belonged now to a new religious group and rejected the Catholic Church. We write, too, in hope and in concern. We are concerned at the harm that error can cause. We are not talking about something theoretical or remote but about people and hearts and minds and lives. It is our hope that you will become more sharply aware of the errors and dangers which these groups present, especially to the young. And finally we pray that the sorrow and challenge we now experience may change us from indifferent and apathetic churchgoers into strong and perfect Christians.

✠ *Joseph*
 Archbishop of Tuam
✠ *Dominic*
 Bishop of Elphin
✠ *Thomas*
 Bishop of Achonry

✠ *Eamonn*
 Bishop of Galway
✠ *Thomas*
 Bishop of Killala
✠ *Joseph*
 Bishop of Clonfert

March, 1983

Appendix II

THE EUROPEAN PARLIAMENT AND CULTS

The European Parliament adopted a Resolution in May 1984 in relation to new religious groups. The resolution embodied a series of recommendations which are listed below:

The European Parliament

Recommends that the following criteria be applied in investigating reviewing and assessing the activity of the above-mentioned orgainsations:

(a) persons under the age of majority should not be forced on becoming a member of an organization to make a solemn long-term commitment that will determine the course of their lives;

(b) there should be an adequate period of reflection on the financial or personal commitment involved;

(c) after joining an organization contacts must be allowed with family and friends;

(d) members who have already commenced a course of education should not be prevented from completing it;

(e) the following rights of the individual must be respected:

— the right to leave an organization unhindered;
— the right to contact family and friends in person or by letter and telephone;

(f) no-one may be incited to break any law, particularly with regard to fund-raising, for example by begging or prostitution;

(g) organizations may not extract permanent commitments from potential recruits, for example students or tourists, who are visitors to a country in which they are not resident;

(h) during recruitment, the name and principles of the organization should always be made immediately clear;

(i) such organisations must inform the competent authorities on request of the address or whereabouts of individual members;

(j) the abovementioned organizations must ensure that individuals dependent on them and working on their behalf receive the social security benefits provided in the member States in which they live or work;

(k) if a member travels abroad in pursuit of the interests of an organization, it must accept responsibility for bringing the individual home, especially in the event of illness;

(i) telephone calls and letters from members' families must be immediately passed on to them;

(m) where recruits have children, organizations must do their utmost to further their education and health, and avoid any circumstances in which the children's well-being might be at risk.

Considers, moreover, a common approach within the context of the Council of Europe to be desirable and calls, therefore, on the governments of the Member States to press for appropriate agreements to be drawn up by the Council of Europe which will guarantee the individual effective protection from possible machinations by these organizations and their physical and mental coercion.

Instructs its President to forward this resolution to the commission and Council of the European Communities, to the Governments and national parliaments of the Member States, and to the Council of Europe.

Bibliography

BROMLEY, David G. and Anson D. Shupe, Jr. *Strange Gods*. Beacon Press, 1981.

BOUDREAU, Albert H. *The Born-Again Catholic*. Living Flame Press. 1980.

BJORNSTAD, James. *The Moon is not the Son*. Bethany Fellowship Inc., 1976.

CLEMENTS, R.D. *God and the Gurus*. Inter-Varsity Press.

CONWAY, Flo and Jim SIEGELMAN. *Snapping*. Dell Publishing Co. Inc., 1979.

DANER, Francine Jeanne. *The American Children of Krishna: A Study of the Hare Krishna Movement*. Rinehart & Winston.

DELLINGER, Robert. *Cults and Kids*. Boys' Town Centre.

EDWARDS, Christopher. *Crazy for God*. Prentice-Hall International, Inc. 1979.

ENROTH, Ronald. *Youth, Brainwashing & the Extremist Cults*. Paternoster Press, 1977.

GARVEY, John. *All Our Sons and Daughters*. Templegate Publishers, 1977.

HOGE, Dean R. *Converts, Dropouts, Returnees*. Pilgrim Press, 1981.

HOPKINS, Joseph. *Children of God – Disciples of Deception*. Christianity Today, 1977.

KERNS, Phil. *People's Temple, People's Tomb*. Logos International.

LANE, Dermot A. *The Experience of God – An Invitation to Do Theology*. Veritas Publications, 1985.

MAHARAJ, Rabindranath R. with Dave HUNT. *Death of a Guru*. Hodder and Stoughton Ltd., 1978.

MARTIN, Walter R. *The Kingdom of the Cults*. Bethany Fellowship, 1965, 1975.

McDOWELL, Josh and Don STEWART. *Understanding the Cults*. Here's Life Publishers Inc., 1982.

MEANS, Pat. *The Mystical Maze*. Campus Crusade for Christ Inc., 1976.

MULLAN, Bob. *Life as Laughter: following Bhagwan Shree Rajnesh.* Routledge & Kegan Paul, 1983.
NEEDLEMAN, Jacob. *The New Religion.* Doubleday & Co., 1972.
O'CONNOR, Edward D., C.S.C. *The Pentecostal Movement in the Catholic Church.* Ave Maria Press, 1971.
PATRICK, Ted with Tom DULACK. *Let Our Children Go!* Ballantine Books, 1976.
PETERSON, Willam J. *Those Curious New Cults.* Keats Publishing, Inc., 1975.
PLOWMAN, Edward E. *The Jesus Movement.* Hodder and Stoughton, 1972.
SARGENT, William. *Battle For The Mind.* Pan Books Ltd., 1975.
SPARKS, Jank. *The Mindbenders.* Thomas Nelson Inc, 1977.
SUENENS, Cardinal. *Ecumenism and Charismatic Renewal: Theological and Pastoral Orientations.* Servant Books, 1978.
TATE WOOD, Allen. *Moonstruck.* Willam Morrow & Co., 1979.
WALLIS, Roy. *The Elementary Forms of The New Religious Life.* Routledge & Kegan Paul, 1984.